THE FUND
AND CHINA
IN THE
INTERNATIONAL
MONETARY
SYSTEM

THE FUND
AND CHINA
IN THE
INTERNATIONAL
MONETARY
SYSTEM

Edited by A.W. Hooke

Papers presented at a colloquium held in
Beijing, China, October 20–28, 1982

International Monetary Fund • 1983

International Standard Book Numbers:
ISBN 0-939934-22-1 (hardcover)
ISBN 0-939934-23-X (softcover)

Foreword

This volume contains the proceedings of a colloquium, jointly sponsored by the People's Bank of China and the International Monetary Fund, that was held in Beijing during October 20–28, 1982. The themes were the role of China and of the Fund in the international monetary system and the outlook for the world economy. Two papers were presented by distinguished economists from leading Chinese universities and seven by the Fund staff. The colloquium was attended by senior officials from government and banking circles, as well as by academics and postgraduate students from a number of universities and institutes throughout China.

The idea of holding the colloquium was conceived during a visit that I was privileged to make to China in October 1981. It became clear to me then that there was a strong desire on the part of Chinese officials, as well as the public at large, to learn more about the structure, policies, and practices of the Fund and to engage in a broader dialogue about the working of the international monetary system. On the part of the Fund, of course, there was a deep interest in China, as well as an imperative need to understand more fully the functioning of the Chinese economy—an economy whose gross domestic product is estimated as the largest in the developing world and the seventh largest among all Fund members.

The colloquium is only one of a series of contacts that have been established between the Chinese authorities and the staff of the Fund in the past three years, as both China and the Fund have set about improving their understanding of each other. In view of the many senior Chinese officials, academics, and students participating in the colloquium and the extent of the formal and informal contacts made, the colloquium was important in the evolution of China's relations with the Fund. It is my hope that publication of these proceedings will contribute to strengthening our mutual interests.

J. DE LAROSIÈRE
Managing Director
International Monetary Fund

April 1983

v

Principal Participants at the Colloquium October 20–28, 1982

Chairman of the Colloquium

SHANG MING — Advisor, People's Bank of China

Presidium of the Colloquium

CHEN DAISUN — Director, Department of Economics, Beijing University

LUO YUANZHENG — Professor, Institute of World Economics and Politics, Academy of Social Sciences

WU DAKUN — Professor, Department of Public Finance, People's University of China

FENG DALIN — Deputy Director, Shaanxi College of Finance and Economics

LIU SHIBAI — Deputy Director, Sichuan College of Finance and Economics

ZHAO HAIKUAN — Director, Research Institute of Finance and Banking, People's Bank of China

TIAN TONGWU — Director, Department of Science and Education, People's Bank of China

YANG PEIXIN — Deputy Director, Research Institute of Finance and Banking, People's Bank of China

GAN PEIGEN — Deputy Director, Research Institute of Finance and Banking, People's Bank of China

HONG MIN — Deputy Director, Department of Foreign Business Administration, People's Bank of China

WANG ENSHAO — Advisor to Executive Director for China, International Monetary Fund

Authors

LUO YUANZHENG   Professor, Institute of World Economics and
                         Politics, Academy of Social Sciences

HONG JUNYAN   Associate Professor, Department of Economics,
                         Beijing University

WM. C. HOOD   Economic Counsellor, and Director, Research
                         Department, International Monetary Fund

AZIZALI MOHAMMED   Director, External Relations Department,
                         International Monetary Fund

LEO VAN HOUTVEN   Secretary, International Monetary Fund

R.J. FAMILTON   Deputy Treasurer, International Monetary
                         Fund

P.R. NARVEKAR   Deputy Director, Asian Department,
                         International Monetary Fund

MANUEL GUITIÁN   Senior Advisor, Exchange and Trade Relations
                         Department, International Monetary Fund

A.W. HOOKE   Editor, External Relations Department,
                         International Monetary Fund

Contents

Page

Foreword v

Principal Participants at the Colloquium vii

Opening Remarks
    Shang Ming.. 1
    Wm. C. Hood 2

The Evolution of the International Monetary System
    and the Changing Role of the Fund
    Azizali Mohammed.................................. 4
    Summary of Discussion.............................. 21

The Framework for Policymaking in the Fund
    Leo Van Houtven 24
    Summary of Discussion.............................. 53

The Current World Economic Situation and the Problem
    of Global Payments Imbalances
    Wm. C. Hood 56
    Summary of Discussion.............................. 71

Some Comments on the Current Economic Situation
    in the West
    Hong Junyan...................................... 74
    Summary of Discussion.............................. 83

The Chinese Economy and Its Role in the World
    Luo Yuanzheng 85
    Summary of Discussion.............................. 94

Page

Fund Programs for Economic Adjustment
  Manuel Guitián 96
  Summary of Discussion 115

Collaboration Between the Fund and the World Bank
  P.R. Narvekar 119
  Summary of Discussion 135

The SDR—An Introduction
  Wm. C. Hood 138
The SDR—Its Evolution and Prospects
  R.J. Familton 146
  Summary of Discussion 161

The Role of the Fund in Developing Countries
  A.W. Hooke 163
  Summary of Discussion 181

Closing Remarks
  Shang Ming 184
  Wm. C. Hood 185
  Azizali Mohammed 186

Opening Remarks

Shang Ming

Ladies, gentlemen, and comrades: I am very pleased to open this colloquium, which is being jointly sponsored by the People's Bank of China and the International Monetary Fund. This marks the first time, since the People's Republic of China resumed its position in the Fund in April 1980, that our two institutions have jointly sponsored such a colloquium. The initiative for it came from Mr. de Larosière, Managing Director of the Fund, when he was visiting China in October–November 1981.

A great deal of preparatory work for the colloquium has been done by our People's Bank and the Fund. I would like to express, on behalf of the People's Bank, our sincere thanks to the speakers from the Fund. Chinese participants include staff of various economic and financial departments and institutions, as well as professors from several distinguished universities and financial and economic colleges in China. Please permit me also, on behalf of the Bank, to extend a warm welcome to all the specialists and comrades attending the meeting. In the past two years, contacts between China and the Fund have increased, and understanding between us has deepened. The present colloquium will, I trust, provide us with another opportunity to deepen our mutual understanding.

During the colloquium, the representatives of the Fund will discuss developments in the international monetary system, the world economic situation, and the role of the Fund in the world economy. The Chinese economists, Professor Luo Yuanzheng and Associate Professor Hong Junyan, will address China's role in the world economy and the current economic situation in the West. Discussions will be held following the speeches.

I believe that, by the end of the colloquium, our understanding of the Fund's policies and its operation will have increased. I hope that the representatives of the Fund will also feel that they have deepened their knowledge of the economic situation in China and of China's economic policies.

I think this colloquium should be regarded as merely the beginning of interchanges between China and the Fund on the policies and operations of that institution. I look forward to further assistance from the Fund in arranging such activities for our mutual benefit. Finally, I wish the colloquium a complete success.

Wm. C. Hood

Mr. Chairman, ladies, and gentlemen: The International Monetary Fund greatly appreciates the opportunity to cosponsor this colloquium with the People's Bank of China—the first opportunity of its kind since the People's Republic of China decided to resume its membership in the Fund and the World Bank.

On behalf of the management of the Fund, we extend greetings to our Chinese hosts. The visit of the Managing Director in late 1981 was designed to provide him with the opportunity to learn about China as well as to explain the Fund. The staff team participating in the colloquium has a similar duty—to explain the complex international organization that is the Fund and to seek to understand the perceptions of Chinese participants about the institution and their own country.

The Fund has experience of centrally planned economies, especially those of Eastern Europe. But it is still in the process of accumulating knowledge and insight into the workings of a centrally planned economy the size of China, an economy that has also embarked on an intensive modernization program using foreign technology, skills, and capital. This promises to be a historic change, not only for China but for the rest of the world and for international organizations like the Fund that have been established to help facilitate international cooperation.

Among these institutions, the Fund is one of the most specialized. It deals with financial matters: it administers a code of conduct in the settlement of payments transactions; it supervises the exchange rate policies of its members; and it provides financial support to members to tide them over temporary difficulties in their external accounts. It has the power to create an internationally accepted reserve asset, the SDR, and has the potential to become a central bank for the world. Finally, it is an international forum, where governments have come together to establish a permanent institution for consultation and for consensus-building among its member countries on matters within the competence of the Fund. In the sessions that follow, the members of the Fund staff team will seek to present these different aspects of the Fund and to understand how they apply to the conditions of a centrally planned economy like China. We look forward to the experience.

The care and efficiency of the preparations made for the colloquium by the Chinese authorities and their Washington representatives, Messrs. Zhang Zicun and Wang Enshao, represent a happy beginning. Success now depends on the frankness and objectivity with which all of us, both the Fund staff and the Chinese participants, approach the program we have before us. We would especially like to express our appreciation to Mr. Shang Ming, Advisor of the People's Bank of China, for the interest that he has evinced in the organization of the colloquium.

The Evolution of the International Monetary System and the Changing Role of the Fund

Azizali Mohammed

The international monetary system comprises a set of arrangements that facilitate the conduct of trading and financial relationships among countries and their residents. For these arrangements to be operated efficiently and to be in the interests of all member countries, a number of rules and conventions observed by governments and their fiscal agencies have evolved in such areas of mutual concern as exchange rates, payments regimes, and reserve assets. The International Monetary Fund, which currently has 146 members, is an intergovernmental institution established by the international community to supervise the working of the international monetary system, to promote the adjustment of payments imbalances, and to serve as a forum for collaboration and for the study and resolution of problems in these areas.

The objectives of the Fund have expanded since it was established in 1945 but still include in essentially unchanged form those written into the original Articles of Agreement. The Fund aims to foster the balanced growth of international trade so as to facilitate the attainment of high levels of real income and employment in member countries and the development of their productive resources. The strategy for achieving these goals includes the promotion of exchange stability, an open and multilateral system of current payments and transfers, and balance of payments adjustment policies that are not detrimental to national or international prosperity. In 1969, the objectives of the Fund were enlarged to cover the growth of international liquidity on a path consistent with the attainment of full employment and price stability through the allocation (or cancellation) of an international reserve asset, the special drawing right (SDR).

This paper discusses the changing role of the Fund against the background of the evolution of the international monetary system. Four aspects of the Fund's activities are analyzed: (1) the trade and payments regime; (2) the exchange rate mechanism; (3) the reserve-creating machinery; and (4) the adjustment process. These elements are, of course, closely interrelated in practice, and their separate treatment is for discussion purposes only. The Fund's evolving role is viewed in relation to each of these elements and as a forum for collaboration and consultation among governments. The paper concludes with a brief review of some of the issues concerning the Fund that are currently occupying the attention of its members.

The Trade and Payments Regime

The trade and payments system that prevailed during most of the 1930s was characterized by the widespread existence of restrictions. Countries were split into numerous trading and currency blocs; trade was channeled through bilateral trade and payments agreements; and there were extensive exchange controls, multiple currency practices, and discrimination. The Fund's founding fathers viewed these arrangements as being shortsighted and detrimental to the outward-looking and cooperative policies necessary for the preservation of political harmony among nations in the postwar period. They also feared that the ending of the war would be followed by an economic slump, as had occurred after World War I, and that this would add to the pressures to resort to restrictive trade and payments policies.

Accordingly, a code of conduct was negotiated at the Bretton Woods Conference in 1944 that attached considerable importance to the attainment of an open and multilateral system of payments and exchange. Members would ensure that payments for current transactions could take place freely and that balances arising out of such transactions could be converted into other currencies. They were to avoid restrictive bilateral and regional payments arrangements and to refrain from multiple currency practices and discriminatory currency arrangements.

Countries in a position to do so were expected to adopt the code on current payments and convertibility as soon as they joined the Fund. It was recognized, however, that because of the dislocations suffered during the war, many countries would not be able to meet this requirement. A transition period was therefore allowed, during which members could retain the restrictions in force at the time they joined the Fund.[1] From March 1952, the Fund was required to consult annually with members still retaining restrictions.

The Fund's code on exchange practices is also based on the premise that there are considerable administrative costs in the maintenance of restrictions. These are especially onerous for countries with scarce administrative resources. The code regards the price mechanism as a sound guide to rational decision making in the areas of international trade and transfers. In fact, it constrains the permanent use of exchange measures to interfere with the working of the price mechanism. This does not mean that governments are expected to accept the economic consequences of the unfettered interplay of market forces. However, adherence to the code does mean that they agree, when they wish to modify the free market result, to do so through the use of other, that is, nonexchange-type, measures. Trade measures are more "transparent" than exchange measures—that is, their effects, particularly the degree of protection they provide, are easier to observe—and are subject to close examination by another international organization established in the postwar period, the General Agreement on Tariffs and Trade.

Examination of the restrictive systems of members and consultations with members about the need to retain restrictions and the means and timing of their removal formed a major part of the Fund's operational work during the 1950s. However, in February 1961, the major European countries joined the United States and Canada in observing the Fund's code on exchange practices, and by the end of that decade, Japan and many developing countries had followed suit.

This broad progress in the liberalization of the exchange system continued in the 1970s. Participation in bilateral payments arrangements and use of multiple currency practices declined. However, restrictions associated with arrears on debt servicing payments emerged as an important problem during the mid-1970s. The number

---

[1] The Second Amendment of the Articles of Agreement gives all new members this privilege without reference to a general transitional period.

of countries in arrears continued to rise, and by the end of 1982 about one fifth of the Fund's membership had payments arrears.

The accumulating arrears are, however, part of a larger problem of external indebtedness, especially of developing countries, and do not represent a reversal of the generalized progress toward a multilateral payments system that has taken place in the postwar period.

The Exchange Rate Mechanism

The origins of the par value system of exchange rates agreed at the Bretton Woods Conference lie in the high costs that were incurred by countries under the gold exchange standard of the late 1920s and that were imposed on countries by the exchange rate measures introduced during the 1930s. The gold standard, with its emphasis on fixed exchange rates and on changes in levels of economic activity as the mechanism for correcting external imbalances, was excessively rigid and forced countries to adjust too abruptly. The exchange rate policies adopted following the collapse of the gold standard, especially the competitive use of devaluation to promote domestic employment, imposed equally heavy burdens, provoking retaliatory measures and causing severe dislocations of world trade.

The par value system incorporated in the Fund's charter was designed to keep rates more stable than during the 1930s but also to allow them to be more adjustable than under the gold standard. Members could change their exchange rate but only to correct a "fundamental disequilibrium" and only after consultation with the Fund and normally with its concurrence. It was widely expected that members would use the exchange rate as one of the instruments of policy.

The par value system appeared to work satisfactorily during the 1950s and the first half of the 1960s. From the mid-1960s, differential rates of economic performance, reflected in divergent rates of inflation, led to payments imbalances in the major industrial countries, which these countries were reluctant to correct by adjusting their exchange rates. Some other countries found that the increasing ease of international capital movements made it impossible to maintain pegged exchange rates, and they adopted "floating" regimes. A series of exchange crises in the late 1960s and early 1970s culminated in the suspension of convertibility for the U.S. dollar in August 1971. By early 1973, most of the major industrial countries had been forced to float their currencies.

Following the breakdown of the par value system, the Committee on Reform of the International Monetary System and Related Issues (Committee of Twenty) was established to advise on exchange rates and other aspects of a reformed international monetary system. The Committee's early efforts focused on the restoration of the par value system with floating in particular situations to be validated and with modifications aimed in part at encouraging members experiencing payments imbalances to adopt early and adequate programs of adjustment, including prompt changes in par values. However, because of large payments imbalances associated with the first oil price rise and increased uncertainty about the future, it soon became apparent that agreement could not be reached on an early return to a par value system. Accordingly, the efforts of the Committee and of its successor, the Interim Committee of the Board of Governors on the International Monetary System (Interim Committee), shifted toward developing a more flexible set of exchange arrangements and of principles that would guide members in the conduct of their exchange rate policies. The results of these deliberations were formalized in the Second Amendment of the Fund's Articles of Agreement that became effective in April 1978.

The rights and obligations of members with respect to exchange arrangements and policies, as specified in the Second Amendment, have three main aspects. First, members are free to choose the form of their arrangement. They may peg the value of their currency to that of another currency, they may peg to a composite or basket of currencies including the SDR, or they may allow the value of their currency to float. They may not, however, peg to gold—a restriction designed to facilitate a reduction in the role of gold in the international monetary system.

Second, members do not have freedom over policies affecting their exchange rate. They have a general obligation to collaborate with the Fund and with each other to promote orderly exchange arrangements and a stable system of exchange rates. They also have the more specific obligation of pursuing economic and financial policies that foster orderly economic growth and reasonable price stability. The focus has thereby been shifted from the stability of the exchange rate to the stability of the underlying conditions. Members are required, however, to eschew exchange rate policies that impede balance of payments adjustment or result in unfair competitive advantage. Members are also expected to intervene in exchange markets to counter disorderly conditions and to take account of the interests of other members in their intervention policies.

Third, the Fund is required to exercise firm surveillance over the exchange rate policies of members. This is conducted in the course of consultations with individual members against the background of the Fund's assessment of the world economic situation and outlook. Exchange rate policy is discussed within the broader framework of other economic and financial policies having a bearing on it and with special attention to the impact on other countries; this latter aspect is naturally stressed in the case of the major industrial countries with a large weight in the world economy. Recently, the interconnections among the principal countries whose currencies are included in the SDR basket (viz., France, the Federal Republic of Germany, Japan, the United Kingdom, and the United States) have been recognized as requiring a special surveillance exercise within a multilateral context, and these countries, together with Canada and Italy, have begun exploring ways of working with the Fund in a more intensive way to achieve a greater convergence of their policies.

The Reserve-Creating Machinery

In the period between the two world wars, the major international reserve assets were gold, pounds sterling, and U.S. dollars. In the negotiations that preceded the Bretton Woods Conference, the United Kingdom recommended that the proposed new international monetary institution be authorized to issue an additional reserve asset. The asset would be transferable among members, and there would be no limit on credit balances. However, the recommendation was opposed by the United States, which feared that it would be required to trade real resources for unlimited holdings of an untried reserve asset. The U.S. view prevailed and, under the original Articles, the Fund was not required to regulate, nor empowered to issue, reserve assets.

With the supply of monetary gold rising slowly, the price of gold in terms of dollars being fixed, and the United Kingdom experiencing balance of payments difficulties that made the pound sterling less attractive as a reserve currency than in earlier periods, the dollar provided the bulk of the increase in reserve assets during the first two decades after World War II. This situation appeared tenable so long as the deficit in the U.S. balance of payments reflected capital movements in the sense that the United States was playing a banker's role— accepting short-term deposits (which other countries regarded as reserves) and lending them out at longer term by way of direct and portfolio investment. However, a dilemma arose if the current rather than the capital account became the major source of the deficits: if these deficits did not continue, international reserves would grow too slowly to maintain world trade and growth at full employment level; if the deficits did continue, confidence in the dollar would be undermined and continuance of its official convertibility doubted. Besides, the system came to be regarded as inequitable since the reserve currency country could acquire real goods and services from abroad in exchange for financial claims on its monetary authorities while other countries had to use reserve assets.

The instability imparted by this currency-based reserve asset system led to a search for an alternative reserve asset. The United States was also becoming concerned about its deteriorating liquidity position vis-à-vis the accumulating short-term dollar liabilities owed to foreign official holders. The Fund's Articles were amended in 1969 to authorize the Fund to create a new asset, the SDR, and the mechanism to allocate SDRs became operative the same year.

The early SDR lacked many of the attributes of a reserve asset. To some extent, it was constructed as an instrument for obtaining credit for a limited number of purposes. There were restrictions on its use, its yield was below that of alternative assets, and heavy users were required to reconstitute their holdings in order to maintain a minimum average level of holdings to allocations over time. These were a reflection of several factors—the need to proceed cautiously with the new asset, the resistance of the United States to an asset that would be too competitive with the dollar, and the desire of some countries to protect the role of gold as a major reserve asset.

In recent years, the characteristics of the SDR have been improved considerably. The Articles of Agreement envisage the SDR as becoming the principal reserve asset of the international monetary system, and, to this end, the Fund has progressively removed restrictions on the use of the SDR, has raised the interest rate on it to the market level, and has abolished the reconstitution requirement. It has also simplified the valuation of the SDR by reducing the number of currencies in the valuation basket from 16 to 5; the valuation and interest rate baskets are now identical. These changes have reflected a strengthening view among most members that the SDR should become a genuine alternative reserve asset.

Annual allocations were made in 1970–72 and again in 1979–81. The total allocation of SDRs so far is 21.4 billion. Members' holdings of SDRs in mid-1982 constituted about 5 percent of their non-gold reserve assets. Clearly, this ratio will have to rise appreciably if the SDR is to become the principal reserve asset in the international monetary system. There is no consensus among Fund members at the present to permit new SDR allocations to be made. The use of the SDR as a unit of account in financial transactions is growing gradually, and its attractiveness as a store of value is enhanced by the increased variability of the exchange rates of the principal reserve currencies, since the SDR, as a composite, tends to vary less than its component currencies.

The Adjustment Process

The changing nature of the Fund's role is perhaps most apparent in its function of promoting balance of payments adjustment. Major aspects of initial funding and lending policies were determined by early 1952, when the view that loans should be conditional on the adoption of satisfactory adjustment programs was accepted and the usefulness of the stand-by arrangement[2] as a framework for the application of conditionality was recognized. These policies were largely unchanged during the following decade, a period when comparatively little use was made of the Fund's resources. However, from 1963, changes occurred at a rapid pace and affected most aspects of the Fund's lending policies, including the specific purposes of loans, the associated policy conditions, the maximum use relative to quota, the duration of disbursement and repayment periods, and the degree of concessionality. These changes also affected the sources that the Fund uses to finance its activities.

---

[2] The stand-by arrangement provides a member with a line of credit that it can draw on in installments during a specified period as long as it adheres to the terms of the arrangement.

Lending

The Fund's early lending policies made no allowances for different types of balance of payments problems. This "one window" approach continued until 1963, when, in recognition of the special difficulties faced by a growing number of primary producing countries, the Fund introduced the compensatory financing facility to assist members coping with payments imbalances attributable to temporary shortfalls in export receipts. A basic innovation of this facility was the recognition that, where the balance of payments problem was of a clearly reversible character and was due largely to circumstances beyond the control of the country, it was unreasonable to expect the country to adjust. The country should have the means to bridge the period until the circumstances creating the problem are reversed. A third lending window was opened in 1969 with the creation of the buffer stock financing facility. This facility, which has been used only occasionally by members, and then for relatively short periods and in small amounts, helps members that have difficulty in financing expenditures associated with the establishment and operation of buffer stock arrangements.

A number of new facilities were established in the mid-1970s. The extended Fund facility was created in 1974 for the purpose of providing resources, in larger amounts and over a longer period of time than under the one-year stand-by arrangement, to countries that either are experiencing balance of payments difficulties of a structural nature or have external positions that are too weak to permit them to undertake an effective development program. This was the fourth regular window opened by the Fund, as distinct from the temporary oil facilities created in 1974 and 1975 to meet the increased costs of oil imports in that period. The latter were designed in part to help members avoid recourse to restrictions and to unduly deflationary demand-management policies following the large rise in oil prices in 1973–74. In 1975, the Fund also established an account to subsidize the interest costs of drawings under the 1975 oil facility by countries most seriously affected by the rise in oil prices.

In the following year, a Trust Fund was created for the purpose of making direct contributions and extending highly concessional loans to low-income developing countries. The Trust Fund was financed out of profits from the sale of a portion of the Fund's gold holdings. In contrast to the origin of other facilities, where the identification of a lending need preceded efforts to establish the facility, the Trust Fund was created following the decision to reduce the size of the Fund's gold holdings as part of the program for gradually demonetizing gold. The subsequent sales of part of the Fund's gold to the public provided the initial funds for setting up the Trust Fund.

There has been a further widening of the range of the Fund's lending facilities in recent years, owing to the larger and more intractable payments imbalances associated with the 1973–74 and 1979–80 rises in the cost of energy. In 1979, the supplementary financing facility was established, and its successor, the enlarged access policy, came into operation in 1981. Both are designed to permit larger access to the Fund than would have been possible under the permanent facilities that were designed to be financed from the quota (or capital) subscription resources of the Fund. In May 1981, the Fund broadened the coverage of the compensatory financing facility to include the provision of assistance to members experiencing temporary increases in the cost of cereal imports.

The concept of Fund conditionality has also evolved over the years. When the Fund was established, it was not even clear that the use of its resources would be subject to policy conditions. In fact, virtually all countries except the United States were initially opposed to the idea. However, it soon became apparent that, if the Fund was to have confidence that the resources it lent would be repaid and be available for the use of other members, it would either have to deny certain requests outright or require that the members adopt policies aimed at correcting their payments imbalances within a definite period. Conditionality practices changed as the Fund gained experience with adjustment programs. The main targets and instruments came to be expressed in quantitative terms in order to make the programs more precise and thus easier to monitor. The practice developed of phasing disbursements over the period of the arrangement. Performance criteria, or tests that determine whether members can continue to draw under stand-by arrangements, were included from 1957.

Until recently, members could borrow from the Fund until the latter's holding of their currency reached 200 percent of quota. Since own-currency subscriptions are at least 75 percent of quota, members could thus draw up to 125 percent of quota.[3] This ceiling could be waived, but only in exceptional circumstances. To start with, the compensatory financing facility did not raise members' total access to Fund resources; drawings made under it reduced potential borrowings under the regular tranche policies by an equal amount. However, the introduction of this facility was accompanied by a relaxation of the approach toward requests for waivers beyond the 200 percent limit, and such requests came to be granted almost automatically. This practice led the Fund to decide, in 1966, to exclude currency holdings resulting from transactions under the compensatory financing facility in determining a member's maximum access under the tranche policies.

The access of members to Fund resources has been increased over the years by extending the exclusion principle to holdings attributable to net drawings under other special facilities (e.g., the oil facilities) and by increasing members' potential access relative to quota. In 1974, access under the extended Fund facility was raised to 140 percent of a member's quota but counting this access from the end of its first credit tranche. In the meantime, however, quotas were declining as a proportion of imports, and the decline became even more pronounced following the second oil price rise in 1979–80. The Fund was clearly in danger of becoming unable to mobilize the "critical mass" of finance necessary to support deficit countries in their adjustment efforts. In mid-1980, the Fund adopted a policy of allowing members implementing strong adjustment programs to draw up to 200 percent of quota in a year. Following the increase of 50 percent in quotas under the Seventh General Review, which became effective at the end of 1980, members can borrow up to 150 percent of quota in a year with a maximum of 450 percent of quota over three successive years. The ceiling on cumulative access is 600 percent of quota. These amounts

---

[3] A drawing that increases the Fund's holdings to no more than 100 percent of a member's quota is a "reserve tranche" transaction that does not have to be repaid. Drawings beyond the quota are credit transactions that have to be repurchased (repaid) and are divided into four tranches, each tranche equal to 25 percent of quota. Thus, drawings that would raise the Fund's holdings beyond 100 percent of quota to 125 percent would be in the first credit tranche. Further drawings would be in the "upper credit tranches" except where certain holdings are excluded under special policies.

are independent of borrowings under the compensatory financing, buffer stock financing, and oil facilities and of scheduled repurchases. They are, of course, also independent of assistance made available through the Trust Fund and the interest subsidy accounts. By liberalizing access in the face of declining quotas and rising payments imbalances, the Fund has demonstrated the importance it attaches to the role of providing adequate financial assistance to countries pursuing appropriate policies of balance of payments adjustment.

The Fund has adapted its disbursement and repayment period to the changing needs of its members. During the 1950s and 1960s, most requests for Fund assistance came from countries with payments deficits that were small relative to their economies and that could be corrected through an appropriate combination of demand-reducing and demand-switching measures. These measures could be implemented quickly and could bring about an early restoration of external balance. Consistent with this situation, disbursement periods were one year or less and repayment periods were three to five years.

With larger current account deficits relative to gross domestic product (GDP) from about the mid-1970s and the frequently structural character of balance of payments problems, it became necessary to lengthen disbursement and repayment periods. The demand for longer disbursement periods was associated with the need to phase the adjustment over a period longer than one year. The disbursement period was set at three years for the extended facility and could reach up to three years in stand-by arrangements as well. The need for longer repayment periods reflected partly the greater time required to eliminate deficits that had increased sharply relative to trade and GDP, as well as the bigger role assigned in the programs to "supply-side" measures, which depended on new investment designed to move resources from the domestic sector into the external sector and on raising internal savings to match the additional investment. The upper limit to the repayment period was set initially at eight years but was subsequently increased to ten years for the extended Fund facility (but was held to seven years for amounts financed from borrowed resources). It was also set at ten years for the Trust Fund; this reflected the concessional nature of Trust Fund loans rather than the nature of the programs these loans supported.

Funding

As noted above, quota subscriptions and borrowings form the basis of Fund resources. A major development of the last two decades has been the relatively slow increase of quotas, and this has been reflected in the growing importance of borrowing as a source of Fund resources since the mid-1970s.

There is widespread agreement among the Fund's membership that quotas should be the main source of the organization's funds. They generate resources from all members and are thus closer to the internationally cooperative character of the institution. Also, these resources have generally been less costly to the Fund than borrowed funds. However, quotas determine not only subscriptions but also potential access to Fund resources, the pattern of SDR allocations, and the distribution of voting power. The determination and ratification of general and selective increases is a time-consuming process, and a large and unexpected rise in the need for resources between quota revisions (which take place every five years at the latest) can be met by borrowing. Furthermore, while quota increases do augment the Fund's resources, they increase by an equal amount its potential liquid liabilities because claims on the Fund held by its creditor members are reserve assets that are immediately encashable in case of balance of payments need. Thus, higher quotas do not improve the balance between available resources and potential demands on the Fund if there is a large difference between the distribution of quotas and the distribution of surpluses among countries.

The Fund's first borrowing arrangement was concluded in 1962 when, under the General Arrangements to Borrow (GAB), ten industrial nations, which subsequently formed the Group of Ten, agreed to lend to the Fund for on-lending to other members of the Group. The interest rate on these borrowings by the Fund, and thus the charges levied by the Fund when it used resources under the GAB, was quite low, in line with the cooperative nature of the Arrangements.

During the 1970s, the Fund borrowed a total amount of SDR 6.9 billion to finance the two oil facilities (now almost entirely repaid) and entered into agreements with 13 industrial and oil exporting countries to borrow the equivalent of SDR 7.8 billion for the supplementary financing facility. Amounts under these agreements have been almost fully committed, except for certain residual amounts arising from stand-by or extended arrangements that have been canceled. In order to finance the current enlarged access policy, the Fund has entered into bilateral borrowing agreements with the Saudi Arabian Monetary Agency for SDR 8 billion and with the Bank for International Settlements and the central banks and official agencies of 18 industrial and developing countries for an additional SDR 1.3 billion.

Further borrowing arrangements will be necessary if the Fund is to meet prospective demands of its members in the period before quotas are increased under the Eighth General Review of Quotas. There is a strong preference among members that borrowings should, as far as possible, be from official sources, but the possibility of a direct approach to the private market is not precluded.[4]

The Fund as a Forum

The Fund's Articles of Agreement require that it provide machinery for members to collaborate and consult on international monetary issues. Many observers regard this as the most important of the Fund's functions and its effectiveness in promoting the clarification and resolution of difficult issues as among the most satisfactory aspects of its work. At present, representatives of 146 countries, with widely differing economic systems, income levels, and patterns of production, discuss and deliberate over a wide range of issues related to individual economies and the international economy. The discussions take place in a collegial atmosphere and with an almost complete absence of rhetoric.

The major forums for consultation and collaboration are the Board of Governors and the Executive Board. The Board of Governors, which normally meets once a year, consists of a representative from each member country, usually its minister of finance or the governor of the

---

[4]On January 18, 1983, the Ministers and Central Bank Governors participating in the GAB announced that they strongly supported a substantial increase of resources available to the Fund and had decided to raise their aggregate credit commitments under the GAB from SDR 6.4 billion to SDR 17 billion. Moreover, the scope of the GAB would be expanded significantly by opening its use to countries other than the GAB participants.

central bank. The Governors have delegated many powers to the Executive Board, which is in continuous session at Fund headquarters in Washington. Most decisions of the Executive Board are taken by consensus rather than on the basis of voting. The Board's work is facilitated by reports prepared by the staff of the Fund, in particular, reports on consultations with member countries in the exercise of surveillance over exchange rates.

The Interim Committee, which was created in 1974, provides an important forum for mobilizing a consensus at the political level. The Committee is an advisory body to the Board of Governors and has the same composition as the Executive Board—its 22 members reflecting the constituency groupings of the Fund. Its members are ministers or central bank governors. It normally meets twice a year—in the spring and at the time of the Annual Meeting of the Board of Governors in the fall. The Articles of Agreement provide for a Council with decision-making powers, but so far no steps have been taken to replace the Interim Committee.

The Next Steps

The issues that currently occupy the attention of member governments of the Fund span all its functions. In the regulatory field, the modalities for the surveillance of exchange rates by the Fund remain under scrutiny. The recent experience with floating exchange rates has demonstrated their inability to wholly insulate the domestic economy from the effects of policies in other countries and has re-emphasized the need for the major industrial countries to pay due regard to the consequences, for their principal trading partners, of their economic policies and, in particular, of the mix of their monetary and fiscal policies. Growing realization of the Fund's potential as a forum is evidenced by the willingness expressed by the seven principal industrial countries at the Versailles summit in June 1982 "to strengthen . . . cooperation with the IMF in its work of surveillance and to develop this on a multilateral basis taking into account particularly the currencies constituting the SDR."[5]

---

[5]"Text of Joint Statement on Monetary Undertakings," *IMF Survey* (Washington), Vol. 11 (June 21, 1982), p. 189.

In the area of the financial role of the Fund, a number of issues are emerging. The fact that no developed country has drawn on the Fund since 1978 has raised questions whether the Fund is not being transformed ineluctably into a development financing agency. The gradual lengthening of the time period of Fund-supported programs has brought it somewhat closer to the interests of its sister institution, the World Bank, which, in turn, has moved its structural lending into some areas of adjustment policy not dissimilar to those of the Fund. A harder question is whether the Fund's conditionality standards need to be modified. A less exacting standard carries the danger of moving the Fund into a "surrogate" donor's role for countries that are really in need of concessional flows to maintain their viability. A more exacting standard might be regarded as contributing to the strains that are already severe in countries seeking to adjust in an environment far more difficult than was envisaged only a short while ago.

Even more complex is the question of the Fund's relationship with the commercial banks, especially in member countries that turn to the Fund for assistance when their normal sources of bank financing are disturbed.

Another set of issues relates to the size of the Fund in the 1980s. It is important that the resources of the Fund be perceived as being adequate to the needs of all its members, including those which have not used the Fund in recent years because of their access to international bank credit. There is also a "systemic" role to be played if large-scale financial turmoil were ever to place at risk an international credit structure built on a vast interbank network and spanning financial centers in a number of countries.[6]

Several new concepts are yet to be explored, such as a Fund based fully on the SDR and the possibility of the Fund's evolving in the direction of a genuine international central banking authority. Many political and economic considerations must be reconciled before decisions can be reached on such questions. What the Fund's record to

---

[6]At a meeting in Washington, D.C., on February 10–11, 1983, the Interim Committee agreed that Fund quotas should be increased under the Eighth General Review of Quotas from about SDR 61 billion to about SDR 90 billion. Forty percent of the overall increase would be distributed to all members in proportion to their existing quotas, and the balance would be distributed in the form of selective adjustments.

date indicates is that the institution has the capacity to respond to changing circumstances in a manner that enables it to play a useful role in the evolution of the international monetary system.

Related Reading

de Vries, Margaret Garritsen, *The International Monetary Fund, 1966–1971: The System Under Stress* (Washington, International Monetary Fund, 1976), 2 vols.

Gold, Joseph, *The Second Amendment of the Fund's Articles of Agreement*, IMF Pamphlet Series, No. 25 (Washington, 1978).

Hooke, A.W., *The International Monetary Fund: Its Evolution, Organization, and Activities*, IMF Pamphlet Series, No. 37, 2nd edition (Washington, 1982).

Horsefield, J. Keith, and others, *The International Monetary Fund, 1945–1965: Twenty Years of International Monetary Cooperation* (Washington, International Monetary Fund, 1969), 3 vols.

International Monetary Fund, *Articles of Agreement* (Washington, 1978).

Summary of Discussion

Participants recognized that the growth of the Fund's membership, particularly the increase in the number of primary producing and developing country members, as well as changing economic circumstances, had led to considerable adaptation of the purposes, policies, and practices of the Fund. Nevertheless, many felt that the Fund could go further toward meeting the needs of its members. In particular, the Fund's surveillance could be strengthened, its financial resources could be enlarged, and its function as a forum could be expanded. Other issues raised were the merits of alternative exchange rate regimes, the relationship between the Fund's prescriptions of rate adjustments and the objective of promoting exchange rate stability, and the likelihood of a return to a fixed exchange rate system.

Under the Second Amendment of its Articles of Agreement, the Fund is required to exercise "firm surveillance" over the exchange rate and related policies of its members. Participants observed, however, that such surveillance had not been effective in producing reasonable stability of exchange rates; in fact, rates among the major currencies had fluctuated much more than would seem to have been required by purely balance of payments considerations. Several argued that this "overshooting" of rates indicated the need for a strengthening of the Fund's surveillance function.

The Fund staff attributed the instability of exchange rates to large changes in underlying conditions owing to, for example, increases in the price of energy, the need to use monetary policies more intensively to moderate the effects of other policies in some countries, and rapid changes in technology, especially communications, as these affected the working of financial markets. They noted that the Fund was endeavoring to strengthen its surveillance through more frequent consultations with members and was experimenting with a multilateral approach. It was encouraging member countries to adopt a more balanced fiscal-monetary policy mix to achieve their aggregate demand targets, rather than to rely on monetary policies alone, and to be more sensitive to the effects of their domestic policies on the economies of other countries. The Fund could not impose operational sanctions on members but did have considerable moral authority in the area of exchange rate policies. Through the quality of its economic analysis and the power of persuasion, the Fund could contribute to the convergence of economic and financial policies among its principal members, thereby promoting a more stable system of exchange rates.

Participants expressed concern about the ability of the Fund to continue to meet the needs of its members for balance of payments assistance on reasonable terms. They pointed out that, particularly in the last decade, there had been a marked fall in the ratio of Fund quotas to current account deficits. Borrowings by the Fund had only partially offset this fall and had increased the cost of Fund resources to members. These developments suggested the need for a substantial increase in quotas.

The Fund staff agreed that the amount of assistance the Fund could make available to members experiencing payments difficulties was important for its function of promoting external adjustment. They explained the concept of the "critical mass" of resources that had to be assembled to assure that appropriate adjustment programs were undertaken and to enable countries to attract additional funds from the international commercial banks and other sources. The Fund had been able to offer larger amounts, relative to quota, under its policy of enlarged access. It was also noted that the Eighth General Review of Quotas was well under way and that other proposals for increasing the Fund's resources were being considered by member countries.

One of the most important, if perhaps also the least discussed, of the Fund's functions was to provide a forum in which members could discuss international monetary problems and explore possible solutions to them. Participants pointed out that the magnitude of such problems had increased sharply in recent years. The decline in the terms of trade of non-oil developing countries, the emergence of debt servicing problems in more than one fourth of these countries, the overshooting of exchange rates, and the intractability of stagflation in the industrial countries were just some examples of these problems. Solutions to such problems required close collaboration and cooperation among countries. The Fund's regular consultations with its member countries as well as the meetings of its governing bodies provided an appropriate framework within which to discuss these problems.

Several participants argued that fluctuations in exchange rates considerably increased the difficulties faced by national authorities in managing international reserves and external debts and by enterprises in making decisions about production and investment in the tradables sector. In view of this, they suggested, it would be useful to explore the possibility of a return to a system of fixed exchange rates. The Fund staff noted that the Second Amendment of the Articles of Agreement provided for the adoption of a par value system by the whole or by a substantial part of the Fund's membership. However, there had been no serious efforts to activate this provision. The prevailing view among the authorities of the major industrial countries seemed to be that, while the experience with floating had been less than satisfactory, a fixed exchange rate system also gave rise to major difficulties. Accordingly, emphasis was being placed on ways of making the present system work more effectively rather than on trying to restore a fixed exchange rate system.

The adjustment programs supported by the use of Fund resources frequently included devaluation of currencies of the members implementing the programs. It was argued that the Fund's support of such measures might be inconsistent with its objective of promoting a stable system of exchange rates. The Fund staff agreed that the Articles of Agreement included the promotion of exchange stability among the purposes of the Fund. They also noted, however, that the Articles enjoined the Fund to "facilitate the expansion and balanced growth of international trade" and argued that, for this purpose, it was stability of real, not nominal, exchange rates that was important. For example, if a country was maintaining a fixed nominal exchange rate and its costs were rising faster than those in the rest of the world, its real exchange rate would be rising and the competitiveness of its export and import-competing sectors would be declining. To protect its foreign trade sector, the country needed to stabilize its real exchange rate by allowing changes in its nominal rate to offset its higher rate of inflation. Such changes would promote an efficient and stable pattern of world trade and would thus be consistent with the purposes of the Fund.

The Framework
for Policymaking in the Fund

Leo Van Houtven

At the Bretton Woods Conference in 1944, the framework for policymaking in the International Monetary Fund was the subject of considerable debate, which reflected the importance both of the tasks that would be assigned to the new institution and of the obligations that its members would undertake. The debate also reflected substantial differences among the conference participants regarding the manner in which they believed the Fund could most effectively function. While the founding fathers could hardly have anticipated the vast changes that would take place in the international political and economic environment and in the international monetary system itself, they succeeded in creating a framework for policymaking that, nearly 40 years later, continues to serve the institution well.

With the creation of the Fund, the members of the international community took the novel and deliberate decision to introduce collective control over the international monetary system. They established for the purpose a code of conduct on international monetary affairs and endowed the institution with a wide-ranging combination of financial, supervisory, and regulatory powers. Fixed exchange rates were the linchpin of the system; they were buttressed by the undertaking of the United States freely to buy and sell gold at the established fixed price. Members subscribed to the code of conduct in the conviction that doing so was the surest way to establish a multilateral system of payments free of exchange restrictions, to facilitate the growth of world trade, and to promote high levels of economic activity and employment.

In the Fund's first 25 years, extraordinary progress was made toward the attainment of these objectives. Sustained economic expansion with relative price stability in most of the 1950s and 1960s led to a kind of economic euphoria in which the prospect of rapid further increases in prosperity was taken for granted and the vicissitudes of the trade cycle appeared to have been brought under control. Members actively collaborated in the Fund with an emphasis on the maintenance of par values, on prompt adjustment of imbalances with Fund assistance, and on the abolition of remaining exchange restrictions.

In the late 1960s, however, the working of the gold exchange standard and the par value system showed signs of stress. In mid-1971, the United States suspended dollar convertibility, and, by early 1973, the par value regime was abandoned. International control over the creation of global liquidity became difficult to maintain, despite the establishment of the special drawing right (SDR) as a new international reserve asset. And, as Fund members became free to choose their own exchange rate regime, new ways had to be found to stabilize the system. Eventually, under the Second Amendment of the Articles of Agreement, effective in 1978, the Fund was given wide-ranging responsibilities of surveillance over members' exchange rate policies. The full and effective exercise of these responsibilities is proving to be a daunting task, and the quest of the founding fathers at Bretton Woods for a stable exchange system thus remains a basic, albeit somewhat elusive, objective of the Fund.

While much of the Fund's attention in the 1970s was devoted to reform of the international monetary system, the issues relating to reform were increasingly overshadowed by developments in the world economy—high and persistent inflation, slow growth and rising unemployment, and renewed pressure for protectionism—that have served as a sharp reminder that the permanence of a liberal international trade and payments regime cannot be taken for granted. Moreover, the need for balance of payments financing grew dramatically after the emergence of massive disequilibria following the rise in oil prices in 1973–74 and again in 1979–80.

The Fund owes its positive record in meeting these challenges to (1) a continuing belief by members that, in an increasingly interdependent world, the Fund is an appropriate and effective forum for reaching decisions on international monetary matters, and (2) a flexible structure and a policymaking process that have enabled the institution to adjust its priorities and activities to a rapidly evolving world economic and monetary environment.

The Structure of the Fund

The Fund consists of the Board of Governors, the Executive Board, the Managing Director, and the staff; it includes, as well, the Interim Committee of the Board of Governors on the International Monetary System, which was created in 1974.[1]

The Board of Governors

The highest-ranking body of the Fund is the Board of Governors, made up of one Governor—usually the minister of finance or central bank governor—and one Alternate from each member country. At the end of 1982, the institution had 146 members, nearly five times the original number in 1945. More than one half of the present members of the Fund were not yet independent nations at the time the Fund was established. Only the U.S.S.R. and a few other independent nations are at present not included in its membership.

The Board of Governors of the Fund customarily meets once a year, usually in late September–early October. Held jointly with the Annual Meeting of the Board of Governors of the World Bank under the chairmanship of a different Governor each year, this Annual Meeting lasts for approximately four days, during which Governors address agenda items in prepared statements that are delivered in open sessions. The meetings are most often convened in the United States in Washington, D.C., the seat of both the Fund and Bank, but it is the custom to change the site every third year when other member countries offer to host the gathering. The choice of site has become increasingly dependent on the host country's ability to house and service the more than 9,000 people attending the meetings in recent

---

[1]It is not intended here to appraise the activities of the Joint Ministerial Committee of the Boards of Governors of the Bank and the Fund on the Transfer of Real Resources to Developing Countries (Development Committee), which was created at the same time as the Interim Committee. The Development Committee concentrates on broad issues concerning the transfer of real resources and on matters within the purview of the World Bank. When the agenda has included matters within the competence of the Fund, these have generally been taken up first by the Interim Committee.

years; but efforts are made to ensure geographical variety, which allows Governors and their delegations an opportunity to improve their understanding of the countries and cultures of their colleagues.

Each member of the Fund is assigned a quota, expressed in SDRs, that broadly reflects its economic size in relation to the total membership of the Fund. The member pays to the Fund a subscription equal to its quota, and, taken together, these subscriptions constitute the primary source of financing of the institution. Quotas determine members' access to the Fund's resources, their share in any allocation of SDRs, and their voting power.

Decision making in the Board of Governors is based on the principle of weighted voting power in relation to quotas.[2] Each member has one vote per SDR 100,000 of its quota; in addition, each member is allotted 250 basic votes. The system of basic votes was devised to raise the share in decision making of the smaller member countries; however, successive general increases in Fund quotas have sharply reduced the share of basic votes. Unless the Articles of Agreement specify a special majority, all decisions of the Board of Governors are taken on the basis of a simple majority of the votes cast. Whatever the required majority, however, the total must include replies from a majority of Governors exercising at least two thirds of the total voting power in the Fund, which is required for a quorum of the Board of Governors.

In the early years of the institution, the Board of Governors was a relatively compact group and was very active in decision making and policy discussions. Because of the dramatic growth in membership and the formal and public character of the meetings, however, it has become increasingly difficult for the Board of Governors to engage in detailed discussion or negotiation of the matters on its agenda. This is left largely to smaller groups meeting in closed session, in particular, the Interim Committee and the Executive Board.

The Executive Board

Consisting at present of 22 Executive Directors meeting under the chairmanship of the Managing Director, the Executive Board is the

---

[2]Annex I lists the current quotas of all members as well as those proposed under the Eighth General Review of Quotas.

central organ of the Fund and is responsible for conducting the business of the institution on a daily basis. The five members with the largest quotas—since 1970, the United States, the United Kingdom, the Federal Republic of Germany, France, and Japan—are each entitled to appoint an Executive Director to serve on the Board, as are the two members whose currencies have been most used in Fund financial transactions in the two-year period preceding the regular election of Executive Directors. These two members are frequently, but not always, among the five with the largest quotas.

Member countries not entitled to appoint an Executive Director form constituencies to elect Directors to the remaining seats on the Board. This process is a political matter left to the members themselves, and, while geographical proximity of countries often facilitates the formation of constituencies, it is by no means the sole consideration. A glance at the various constituencies formed over the years shows that members with very different economic and political structures and levels of development have frequently joined forces to elect a Director to the Board.

An Executive Director who is appointed to the Board serves at the pleasure of the government that appoints him; an elected Director serves for a two-year term, although there is no limit on the number of times he may be re-elected. Each Director appoints an Alternate and selects assistants to help him deal with the tasks of the office.

The first Executive Board included 12 Directors, with 5 appointed and 7 elected by the 38 members at the Inaugural Meeting in 1946. As the membership of the institution grew, the size of the Executive Board was gradually increased to 20 in 1964, when the Fund had 93 members. This development led to rising concern about the appropriate size and structure of the Executive Board and the maintenance of a reasonable geographical balance in its composition. Because of this concern, the size of the Board was held to 20 Directors between 1964 and 1978—although the membership of the institution increased by 37 countries during that period—and major shifts in geographical composition of the Board were avoided.

The size of the Board was increased to 21 in 1978, when Saudi Arabia became entitled to appoint an Executive Director because the Saudi Arabian riyal was one of the two currencies that had been most used in Fund transactions in the preceding two years. Under the same provision, Saudi Arabia also appointed an Executive Director in 1980 and in 1982. Another seat was added to the Executive Board in 1980 when the Government of the People's Republic of China assumed the representation of China with a quota that made it possible for China to elect an Executive Director by itself without forming a constituency with other members. At present, 7 Directors on the Executive Board are from Western Europe, 5 from Asia and Australia, 3 from Latin America, 3 from the Middle East, 2 from North America, and 2 from sub-Saharan Africa.[3]

The principle of weighted voting applicable to the Board of Governors also applies to the Executive Board. An elected Executive Director, however, may not split his vote, even if the members of the constituency that have elected him hold differing views on a particular issue. An elected Director may place those differing views on the record, but he may cast his vote only as a unit.

The nature of the body that would be charged with the conduct of the day-to-day operations of the Fund was an issue of some controversy at the time of the negotiation of the Agreement in 1944. Some participants, like the United Kingdom, held the view that the Executive Board should be composed of top-ranking officials— including perhaps governors with political responsibility—who would continue to function in national capitals and travel to headquarters to attend meetings of the Executive Board as and when the business of the Fund required. Others, like the United States, argued that the Executive Board should be a body of experts that would be available at headquarters to meet in continuous session. Those favoring the former approach perceived a need for political control by national capitals over Fund policies and operations; those preferring the latter approach considered that the tasks of the Board would be so wide-ranging and complex that its Directors should devote their full time to them. While it was finally agreed that the Board would be a body of experts meeting in continuous session, the question of political control of the institution by its member governments has arisen time and again and was certainly one reason behind the formation of certain groups of Fund members as well as the establishment of the Committee of Twenty and the Interim Committee, developments that are dealt with later in this paper.

---

[3]Annex II lists the Executive Directors on March 21, 1983 together with the members that have appointed or elected them and their voting power.

The Managing Director and the staff

The Managing Director is the Chairman of the Executive Board and the head of the staff. Appointed by the Executive Board for a five-year term that can be extended or renewed, the Managing Director must, upon his appointment, resign from other positions he may be holding because, like all members of the staff, he owes his allegiance entirely to the Fund.

As head of the institution, the Managing Director often presents his views on international monetary affairs and issues of interest to the Fund. The public addresses by the Managing Director have evolved into an important channel for communicating to the international financial community the Fund's position on current policy issues with which the institution is concerned. In addition, in private meetings, the Managing Director has an opportunity to hold frank and authoritative exchanges of view with heads of state, governors, and ministers of member countries.

As head of the staff, the Managing Director is assisted by a Deputy Managing Director and by the department heads, who at present number 15. Most departments in the Fund fall into one of three categories: area departments, which are concerned mainly with relations with member countries; functional departments, which are concerned primarily with the institution's policies and operations; or service departments, including those which provide technical assistance to members. Over the years, a high-quality staff has been recruited from as wide a geographical basis as possible, and considerable efforts have been made to limit the overall size of the staff (approximately 1,600 at present) and to maintain a short chain of command in order to promote operational efficiency.

The Interim Committee

The Interim Committee of the Board of Governors on the International Monetary System is a forum in which issues concerning the management and adaptation of the system can be discussed on a more political level than in the Executive Board and more efficiently than in the Board of Governors. Established in 1974, the Interim Committee duplicates the structure of the Executive Board, except that its 22 members are governors, ministers, or others of comparable rank and it acts in an advisory rather than a decision-making capacity. Each member of the Interim Committee may be assisted by a number of associates, plus the relevant Executive Director.

The Interim Committee selects its chairman. Thus far, all chairmen have been selected for no fixed term from among the members of the Committee, although each has taken the initiative of resigning from the chairmanship when he ceased to be a member. The Managing Director is a participant in the meetings of the Committee. Based on the preparatory work of the Executive Board, the agenda of the Interim Committee is prepared by the Chairman in consultation with the Managing Director; reports by the Executive Board or the Managing Director usually serve as the basis for discussion of agenda items.

In recent years, the Interim Committee has met twice a year, usually once in the spring and again in the fall, immediately prior to the Annual Meeting of the Board of Governors.[4] The meetings, which usually last one to one and a half days, are not open to the public; nevertheless, taking into account associates, observers, and senior staff of the Fund, total attendance at these meetings often exceeds 250. Despite the size of the meetings and the complexity or political nature of many agenda items, the Committee has not resorted to working parties or subgroups. The 22 members of the Committee, however, may meet with the Chairman and the Managing Director in restricted session—sometimes informally over lunch or dinner—in order to resolve particularly difficult issues and to prepare their guidance for the Executive Board. Still, all agenda items, including the preparation of the press communiqué, are concluded formally in regular sessions.

The Policymaking Process

The functioning of the Board of Governors

The power of the Fund flows from the Board of Governors, and that body has delegated to the Executive Board all decision-making powers except those expressly reserved for itself in the Articles of Agreement, such as the admittance of new members, changes in quotas, allocations of SDRs and certain other matters relating to SDRs, amendment of the

---

[4]The Committee held its twentieth meeting in February 1983.

Articles, and, if necessary, the review of decisions of the Executive Board.

Any matter, however, can be placed on the agenda of the Board of Governors at the request of a Governor, the Managing Director, or the Executive Board. When such matters require a decision, proposed resolutions are submitted for a formal vote by Governors. The resolutions are usually adopted without objection, a consensus on the issues having been reached at the level of the Interim Committee or the Executive Board. Between meetings, any matter requiring a vote by the Board of Governors is handled by mail.

In the 1960s and early 1970s, a number of major proposals on the issues of international liquidity, the working of the exchange system, and other aspects of monetary reform were put forward at the Annual Meetings. In more recent years, the Governors have focused their attention on the world economic outlook, the adjustment process, and the financing of payments imbalances. Also, a number of Governors—particularly those from the developing countries—have used the Annual Meetings to highlight the special problems of their countries and to press their call for a new international economic order.

Delegations from member countries prepare for the Annual Meetings of the Board of Governors (as well as for meetings of the Interim Committee) in a number of regional and group meetings and caucuses of constituencies. The regional meetings include those of the finance ministers and central bank governors of the European Community, the Commonwealth countries, Latin America, the French franc area, Africa, and Asia. The industrial countries coordinate their views in the Group of Ten or in smaller groups, and the developing countries prepare their position in the Group of Twenty-Four.

The joint Annual Meetings of the Fund and the World Bank are the largest periodic gathering of finance ministers, central bank governors, and other senior economic policymakers in the world. Today, they attract great interest from the press—which gives them worldwide coverage—and from the international banking and financial community, whose representatives are invited to attend the meetings. Other international organizations often take advantage of the presence of officials at the Annual Meetings to call working sessions of their own. The number of people in attendance at the meetings and the variety of financial business conducted during the week may, on occasion, even appear to detract from the deliberations of the Boards of Governors. In that respect, the Annual Meetings should be seen in a wider context than in the past: they provide a unique forum in which worldwide monetary cooperation—a fundamental goal of the Fund—can be fostered.

The functioning of the Executive Board

In dealing with the day-to-day business of the Fund, the Executive Board meets in continuous session at headquarters in Washington, D.C. The term "in continuous session" means that the members of the Executive Board must be available to meet at any time on matters of concern to the Fund. In fact, the Board holds formal meetings as and when its work requires. On average, it meets three times a week, often both morning and afternoon, with more frequent meetings in periods of intense operational activity, for example, in advance of scheduled meetings of the Board of Governors and the Interim Committee.

Under the direction of the Managing Director, the staff of the Fund prepares the documentation for the Executive Board. Although reviewed and approved by the Managing Director, papers are generally submitted to the Board as staff memoranda rather than as memoranda from the Managing Director. This practice has served to encourage a freer debate in the Executive Board and to give greater flexibility to the Managing Director in "steering" the Board toward a position that will find broad support or in formulating compromise proposals. Staff papers on substantive issues are circulated to the Executive Board three or four weeks in advance of their consideration;[5] this procedure gives Directors time to study the documentation as well as an opportunity to seek comments or instructions from national capitals and to exchange views informally with other Directors, the management, and the staff.

As noted earlier, all decisions of the Fund are to be taken by a simple majority of the votes cast, unless the Articles provide for a special higher majority. An Executive Director may request a formal vote on any agenda item, but this right has seldom been exercised. Instead, since the early days of the Fund, decisions have ordinarily been adopted

---

[5]Shorter periods may apply for operational reasons or for routine business. In addition, a large number of matters are dealt with on a lapse-of-time basis—that is, in the absence of objection by an Executive Director within a specified time, it being understood that any Director may request that a matter be placed on the agenda.

on the basis of the sense of the meeting as ascertained by the Chairman rather than through a formal vote. The sense of the meeting has been defined as "a position supported by Executive Directors having sufficient votes to carry the question if a vote were taken." Thus, the Board makes a painstaking effort to find common ground, and the weight and logic of a speaker's argument on a given issue—whatever his voting power—can be effective in swaying others to compromise. The Executive Directors are not subject to a time constraint in expressing their positions, reservations, or questions, and the Chairman normally defers ascertaining the sense of the meeting until all who wish to speak have done so, including often a second or third time in response to arguments of others. While decision making by consensus thus tends to encourage a greater number of speakers and longer and more frequent interventions, the decisions that finally result from this thorough review of the issues may well be the best possible decisions that can be taken.

The Executive Board's effort to reach a consensus on the matters before it is clearly reflected in the minutes of Board meetings, which provide a detailed record of the policy history of the Fund and include the interventions of Directors, the Chairman, and the staff, the Chairman's formal summing up at the conclusion of consultation discussions, discussions on important policy matters, and the texts of decisions adopted by the Board.

The Executive Board has tended to avoid extensive use of committees as an aid in the decision-making process. The feeling has always been that such an approach might lead to fractionalization of the Board, which could interfere with the taking of decisions by consensus. There are, of course, a few standing committees, which consider specific matters and submit reports and recommendations to the Executive Board; however, the meetings of these committees are open to participation by all Directors, and there is no presumption that the recommendations of the committees will necessarily be accepted by the Board.

Informal consultations among Executive Directors before agenda items are taken up in the Board have become an intrinsic part of the work methods of Directors. These consultations include, for instance, periodic meetings of Executive Directors of the European Community countries, the Group of Ten industrial countries, and the developing countries. The Managing Director and senior staff are always available for informal discussions with Executive Directors; and the Managing Director often initiates such meetings with Board members, either individuals or groups, to seek their views on confidential or particularly sensitive matters.

In any appraisal of the policymaking process in the Fund, it is crucial to recognize the Executive Board as a college of officials who devote their full time to the affairs of the institution. Free debate in the Board and continuous consultation among Board members, as well as with their authorities and with the management and staff, ensure a thorough examination of the often complex issues, thereby opening avenues toward their resolution.

While the Managing Director has no voting power in the Executive Board (except in the unlikely event of a tie), his stature as head of the institution adds weight to his interventions in meetings; and Directors look to him for guidance on the issues and for formulating acceptable compromises. Also influential in the outcome of discussions are staff members who are called on to defend staff recommendations and respond to questions. Decision making in the Fund is a complex process of interaction between the Executive Directors, the Managing Director, and the staff. And the fact that all participants "live under the same roof" at headquarters has had a most beneficial effect on policymaking by stimulating a strong sense of collegiality and promoting understanding of differing viewpoints, thus facilitating the search for consensus.

Since the mid-1960s, the work load of the Board has grown to a level that has placed increasingly heavy demands on Executive Directors attempting to do full justice to all the matters on the Board's agenda. Issues relating to international liquidity, the creation of the SDR regime, and successive exchange rate crises commanded much of the Board's attention in the late 1960s and early 1970s, as did the search for comprehensive monetary reform. In the mid-1970s, the Board was entrusted with the vast task of negotiating the Second Amendment of the Articles of Agreement.

At the same time, following the first round of oil price increases in late 1973, dramatic changes in the structure of imbalances in international payments and increased calls by members for the use of Fund resources created additional work for the Board as part of the effort to expand the scope of existing facilities or create new ones to meet the needs of members. The agenda of the Executive Board has continued to expand as the worldwide recession of recent years has exacerbated the balance of payments problems of members and as more adjustment programs have had to be negotiated. Another major task of the Executive Board is the need to hold periodic consultations with member countries. These have become an important element in the exercise by the Fund of its surveillance function. In order to deal with this extraordinary expansion of the agenda, more systematic programming of the Board's work has been initiated with periodic forecasting of the work schedule, often for several months ahead, which allows the Board to determine its priorities and set appropriate deadlines for the discussion or resolution of issues.

The Influence of Groups of Members in the Policymaking Process

Since the establishment of the Fund, members have searched for ways of enhancing their influence in the policymaking process or of ensuring that their needs and concerns would be met by the policies and decisions of the institution. One successful approach has been the formation of groups of members. During the 1960s and 1970s, two such groups were formed that have had a profound impact on policymaking in the Fund.

The Group of Ten

The Group of Ten came into being as a result of the Fund's initiative in the early 1960s to supplement its liquidity by borrowing from members in strong external positions. The participants in the so-called General Arrangements to Borrow were the Fund's main industrial member countries or their central banks.[6] Commanding a voting majority in the Fund, the Group of Ten aroused particular concern in the following decade by attempting through its activities to shift decision-making responsibility, particularly in the areas of international liquidity and of exchange rates, away from the Fund and its

---

[6]Belgium, Canada, France, the Deutsche Bundesbank (Federal Republic of Germany), Italy, Japan, the Netherlands, the Sveriges Riksbank (Sweden), the United Kingdom, and the United States. Subsequently, Switzerland was associated with the General Arrangements to Borrow.

Executive Board. The Group of Ten members believed that they—or a similar small group of strong currency members—should assume responsibility for creating and managing reserve currencies.

The Fund, on the other hand, stressed that questions of the adequacy and creation of international liquidity should be matters for the collective judgment of the international community and should not be determined only by a group of industrial countries, particularly when it was mainly the developing countries that needed both increased transfers of real resources and additional international liquidity. Fund Governors thoroughly discussed both sides of the issue at the Annual Meetings, and among the various speakers, the Managing Director himself made it clear that he was opposed to anything but a universal approach through the Fund.

In late 1967 and early 1968, an unprecedented set of four joint meetings were held between the Deputies of the Group of Ten and the Executive Board; these meetings gave both sides the opportunity to explain and clarify their thinking. The universal approach to the creation of international liquidity through the Fund was gradually accepted because it was deemed more "legitimate" (a frequently used term in the discussions) and because it was realized that the strains on international relations resulting from a more limited approach would outweigh its possible advantages. Subsequently, the Group of Ten's lack of success in the late 1960s and early 1970s in dealing with the successive exchange rate crises among the major currencies further strengthened the view that the management and reform of the international monetary system should be carried out within the Fund.

The Group of Twenty-Four

At the time of the first meeting of the United Nations Conference on Trade and Development in 1964, the Group of Seventy-Seven was established to provide a forum on international monetary affairs in which the economic interests of the developing countries could be represented. In 1971, the Group of Seventy-Seven itself set up an Intergovernmental Group of Twenty-Four on International Monetary Affairs, with the African, Asian, and Latin American regions each appointing eight members of the Group at the ministerial and deputy level. The work of the Group of Twenty-Four was originally geared toward ensuring a systematic consideration of the interests and concerns of the developing countries by the Committee of Twenty; when the Committee of Twenty concluded its work in 1974, the Group of Twenty-Four directed its attention to the activities of the Interim Committee.

In 1979, the Group of Twenty-Four prepared an "Outline for a Program of Action on International Monetary Reform," which was submitted to the Interim and Development Committees and to the Boards of Governors of the Fund and the World Bank. Several of the recommendations contained therein have since been implemented and others are pending. The Program of Action of the Group of Twenty-Four has thus, to a considerable extent, become part of the work program of the Fund, which is indicative of the recognition and influence of the Group as the voice of the developing countries in international monetary affairs.

Adaptations in the Structure of the Institution

In forming high-level groups, members of the Fund were attempting to fulfill what many of them had long perceived to be a need to deal effectively on a high-ranking and political level with certain important policy issues facing the institution. In the early years of the Fund, when the total membership had been small, the Board of Governors might have been able to discuss and resolve such matters on a ministerial level. But the membership of the Fund increased dramatically, as did the attendance at the Annual Meetings of the Board of Governors, and it gradually became evident to some members that a more restricted high-level forum was needed, particularly for the conduct of negotiations toward comprehensive monetary reform that was called for in the wake of the breakdown of the Bretton Woods system. This belief rekindled the 1944 debate on the appropriate framework for dealing with international monetary matters and again raised questions about whether the Executive Board or a more political body should be mainly responsible for decision making. Following long and arduous discussions of the issue, it was finally agreed (1) that international monetary matters should continue to be resolved within the Fund and (2) that it would be counterproductive to create an advisory committee or decision-making body of governors that would weaken the authority of the Executive Board.

The Committee of Twenty

In July 1972, the Board of Governors established the Committee of Twenty, that is, the ad hoc advisory Committee of the Board of Governors on Reform of the International Monetary System and Related Issues. After further lengthy negotiations, it was decided that the membership composition of the Committee should parallel that of the Executive Board, which at that time had 20 Directors, although members would be governors, ministers, or others of comparable rank. It was also agreed that the work of the Committee would be prepared by Deputies—rather than by the Executive Board—with the assistance of the Fund staff. The Chairman of the Deputies would be assisted by four Vice-Chairmen chosen from different geographical regions; together they formed the Bureau, which managed the work of the Deputies.

The task of the Committee was to advise the Board of Governors on all aspects of the reform of the system, including proposals for amendment of the Articles of Agreement. The principal issues before the Committee were (1) balance of payments adjustment, (2) the settlement of payments imbalances, (3) global liquidity (including SDRs and consolidation), and (4) the special problems of developing countries.

Progress in the work of the Committee was slow, not only because of the complexity of the subjects to be discussed, but also because few participants had developed coherent positions on all the major issues. This situation contrasted sharply with that at the Bretton Woods Conference, which had been dominated by the comprehensive proposals of the United States and the United Kingdom, and the contrast vividly illustrates the evolution that had occurred by the early 1970s toward a multipolar world in which the developing countries were playing an increasingly influential role.

With the dramatic rise in oil prices in 1973–74, it became apparent that plans for monetary reform were being fundamentally affected by new and urgent economic problems and the vastly changed prospects for the global balance of payments structure. In its final report of June 1974, the Committee therefore withdrew its earlier objective of a "blueprint" or "grand design" for monetary reform, which it concluded would have to be an evolutionary process. The Committee nonetheless identified a number of reform proposals for "early implementation" by the Fund. In doing so, it set the stage for a four-year effort by the Executive Board to prepare for the Second Amendment of the Articles of Agreement and called for the establishment of an Interim Committee at ministerial level in the Fund.

The Interim Committee

The Interim Committee of the Board of Governors on the International Monetary System was established promptly after the dissolution of the Committee of Twenty. The principal task of the Interim Committee was—and is—to advise the Board of Governors with respect to the management and adaptation of the international monetary system, and many of the constitutional and procedural features of the Committee are similar to those of its predecessor.

In its first eight years, the Committee has reviewed (1) outstanding questions relating to the Second Amendment, including the exchange rate regime and the role of gold; (2) the Sixth, Seventh, and Eighth General Reviews of Quotas; (3) new financing facilities in the Fund and policies on the use of Fund resources; (4) a substitution account; and (5) the Fund's liquidity and borrowing needs. Discussions on operational matters usually take place in conjunction with the Committee's review of the world economic outlook, which has assumed increasing importance in recent years because of the Fund's responsibility for exercising firm surveillance over exchange rates.

Under the amended Articles, the Governors can decide, by an 85 percent majority of the voting power in the institution, to replace the Interim Committee, which has an advisory function, with a decision-making Council of the Board of Governors. The terms of reference and the procedural arrangements of the Council would be basically the same as those of the Interim Committee, except that each member would be able to cast separately the votes of each country of his constituency.

There has, thus far, not been much pressure to convert the Committee into a Council. There are indications that many of the developing countries would resist any pressure toward conversion out of a concern that they would have less influence in a Council—where decisions would be taken on the basis of weighted voting—than in an advisory group such as the Interim Committee in which the members representing the developing countries number half of the total of 22 participants. Resistance would probably also be evidenced by those concerned that the creation of a Council could weaken the authority of the Executive Board. Besides, the experience with the Interim Committee, as a political body, has thus far been quite positive: its deliberations have been cordial and businesslike, and the guidance it has given to the Executive Board has reflected a continuing recognition by members of the interdependence of nations.

*   *   *

Because sovereignty over domestic and external monetary affairs has always been a strongly defended prerogative of national governments, the very thought of creating an institution for managing and supervising the international monetary system was innovative; the actual establishment of the Fund and the effort of members to ensure its effectiveness must be described as remarkable. The international monetary system of today differs substantially from the one that was conceived at the Bretton Woods Conference in 1944. Both the international economy and the community of nations have evolved into a multipolar interdependent world in which the developing countries are playing an increasing role. The ability of the Fund to respond to such changes and to face the challenges created by them has been due in large part to the willingness of members to exercise flexibility in working together toward common objectives within a strong but adaptable institutional framework.

Annex I

Current Fund Quotas and Quotas Proposed Under the Eighth General Review

Member	Current Quota	Proposed Quota
	(In millions of SDRs)	
Afghanistan	67.5	86.7
Algeria	427.5	623.1
Antigua and Barbuda	3.6	5.0
Argentina	802.5	1,113.0
Australia	1,185.0	1,619.2
Austria	495.0	775.6
Bahamas	49.5	66.4
Bahrain	30.0	48.9
Bangladesh	228.0	287.5
Barbados	25.5	34.1
Belgium	1,335.0	2,080.4
Belize	7.2	9.5
Benin	24.0	31.3
Bhutan	1.7	2.5
Bolivia	67.5	90.7
Botswana	13.5	22.1
Brazil	997.5	1,461.3
Burma	109.5	137.0
Burundi	34.5	42.7
Cameroon	67.5	92.7
Canada	2,035.5	2,941.0
Cape Verde	3.0	4.5
Central African Republic	24.0	30.4
Chad	24.0	30.6
Chile	325.5	440.5
China	1,800.0	2,390.9
Colombia	289.5	394.2
Comoros	3.5	4.5
Congo	25.5	37.3
Costa Rica	61.5	84.1

Member	Current Quota	Proposed Quota
	(In millions of SDRs)	
Cyprus	51.0	69.7
Denmark	465.0	711.0
Djibouti	5.7	8.0
Dominica	2.9	4.0
Dominican Republic	82.5	112.1
Ecuador	105.0	150.7
Egypt	342.0	463.4
El Salvador	64.5	89.0
Equatorial Guinea	15.0	18.4
Ethiopia	54.0	70.6
Fiji	27.0	36.5
Finland	393.0	574.9
France	2,878.5	4,482.8
Gabon	45.0	73.1
Gambia, The	13.5	17.1
Germany, Federal Republic of	3,234.0	5,403.7
Ghana	159.0	204.5
Greece	277.5	399.9
Grenada	4.5	6.0
Guatemala	76.5	108.0
Guinea	45.0	57.9
Guinea-Bissau	5.9	7.5
Guyana	37.5	49.2
Haiti	34.5	44.1
Honduras	51.0	67.8
Hungary	375.0	530.7
Iceland	43.5	59.6
India	1,717.5	2,207.7
Indonesia	720.0	1,009.7
Iran, Islamic Republic of	660.0	1,117.4
Iraq	234.1	504.0
Ireland	232.5	343.4
Israel	307.5	446.6
Italy	1,860.0	2,909.1
Ivory Coast	114.0	165.5

Member	Current Quota	Proposed Quota
	(In millions of SDRs)	
Jamaica	111.0	145.5
Japan	2,488.5	4,223.3
Jordan	45.0	73.9
Kampuchea, Democratic	25.0	25.0
Kenya	103.5	142.0
Korea	255.9	462.8
Kuwait	393.3	635.3
Lao People's Democratic Republic	24.0	29.3
Lebanon	27.9	78.7
Lesotho	10.5	15.1
Liberia	55.5	71.3
Libya	298.4	515.7
Luxembourg	46.5	77.0
Madagascar	51.0	66.4
Malawi	28.5	37.2
Malaysia	379.5	550.6
Maldives	1.4	2.0
Mali	40.5	50.8
Malta	30.0	45.1
Mauritania	25.5	33.9
Mauritius	40.5	53.6
Mexico	802.5	1,165.5
Morocco	225.0	306.6
Nepal	28.5	37.3
Netherlands	1,422.0	2,264.8
New Zealand	348.0	461.6
Nicaragua	51.0	68.2
Niger	24.0	33.7
Nigeria	540.0	849.5
Norway	442.5	699.0
Oman	30.0	63.1
Pakistan	427.5	546.3
Panama	67.5	102.2
Papua New Guinea	45.0	65.9
Paraguay	34.5	48.4

Member	Current Quota	Proposed Quota
	(In millions of SDRs)	
Peru	246.0	330.9
Philippines	315.0	440.4
Portugal	258.0	376.6
Qatar	66.2	114.9
Romania	367.5	523.4
Rwanda	34.5	43.8
St. Lucia	5.4	7.5
St. Vincent and the Grenadines	2.6	4.0
São Tomé and Principe	3.0	4.0
Saudi Arabia	2,100.0	3,202.4
Senegal	63.0	85.1
Seychelles	2.0	3.0
Sierra Leone	46.5	57.9
Singapore	92.4	250.2
Solomon Islands	3.2	5.0
Somalia	34.5	44.2
South Africa	636.0	915.7
Spain	835.5	1,286.0
Sri Lanka	178.5	223.1
Sudan	132.0	169.7
Suriname	37.5	49.3
Swaziland	18.0	24.7
Sweden	675.0	1,064.3
Syrian Arab Republic	94.5	139.1
Tanzania	82.5	107.0
Thailand	271.5	386.6
Togo	28.5	38.4
Trinidad and Tobago	123.0	170.1
Tunisia	94.5	138.2
Turkey	300.0	429.1
Uganda	75.0	99.6
United Arab Emirates	202.6	385.9
United Kingdom	4,387.5	6,194.0
United States	12,607.5	17,918.3
Upper Volta	24.0	31.6

Member	Current Quota	Proposed Quota
	(In millions of SDRs)	
Uruguay	126.0	163.8
Vanuatu	6.9	9.0
Venezuela	990.0	1,371.5
Viet Nam	135.0	176.8
Western Samoa	4.5	6.0
Yemen Arab Republic	19.5	43.3
Yemen, People's Democratic Republic of	61.5	77.2
Yugoslavia	415.5	613.0
Zaïre	228.0	291.0
Zambia	211.5	270.3
Zimbabwe	150.0	191.0
Total	61,059.8	90,034.8

Annex II

Executive Directors, Their Constituencies, and Voting Power in the Fund on March 21, 1983

Director *Alternate*	Casting Votes of	Votes by Country and Con- stituency[1]	Percent of Fund Total[2]
APPOINTED			
Richard D. Erb *Charles H. Dallara*	United States	126,325	19.52
John Anson *Christopher T. Taylor*	United Kingdom	44,125	6.82
Gerhard Laske *Guenter Grosche*	Germany, Fed. Rep. of	32,590	5.04
Bruno de Maulde *Anne Le Lorier*	France	29,035	4.49
Teruo Hirao *Tadaie Yamashita*	Japan	25,135	3.88
Yusuf A. Nimatallah *Jobarah E. Suraisry*	Saudi Arabia	21,250	3.28
ELECTED			
Miguel A. Senior (Venezuela) *José L. Feito (Spain)*	Costa Rica El Salvador Guatemala Honduras Mexico Nicaragua Spain Venezuela	865 895 1,015 760 8,275 760 8,605 10,150 ――――― 31,325	4.84

Director *Alternate*	Casting Votes of	Votes by Country and Con- stituency[1]	Percent of Fund Total[2]
ELECTED (continued)			
Robert K. Joyce (Canada)	Antigua and Barbuda	286	
Michael Casey (Ireland)	Bahamas	745	
	Barbados	505	
	Belize	322	
	Canada	20,605	
	Dominica	279	
	Grenada	295	
	Ireland	2,575	
	Jamaica	1,360	
	St. Lucia	304	
	St. Vincent and the Grenadines	276	
		27,552	4.26
J.J. Polak (Netherlands)	Cyprus	760	
Tom de Vries	Israel	3,325	
(Netherlands)	Netherlands	14,470	
	Romania	3,925	
	Yugoslavia	4,405	
		26,885	4.15
Jacques de Groote (Belgium)	Austria	5,200	
Heinrich G. Schneider	Belgium	13,600	
(Austria)	Hungary	4,000	
	Luxembourg	715	
	Turkey	3,250	
		26,765	4.14
Giovanni Lovato (Italy)	Greece	3,025	
Costa P. Caranicas	Italy	18,850	
(Greece)	Malta	550	
	Portugal	2,830	
		25,255	3.90

Director *Alternate*	Casting Votes of	Votes by Country and Con- stituency[1]	Percent of Fund Total[2]
ELECTED (continued)			
A.R.G. Prowse	Australia	12,100	
(Australia)	Korea	2,809	
Kerry G. Morrell	New Zealand	3,730	
(New Zealand)	Papua New Guinea	700	
	Philippines	3,400	
	Seychelles	270	
	Solomon Islands	282	
	Vanuatu	319	
	Western Samoa	295	
		23,905	3.69
Mohamed Finaish (Libya)	Bahrain	550	
Tariq Alhaimus (Iraq)	Iraq	2,591	
	Jordan	700	
	Kuwait	4,183	
	Lebanon	529	
	Libya	3,234	
	Maldives	264	
	Oman	550	
	Pakistan	4,525	
	Qatar	912	
	Somalia	595	
	Syrian Arab Republic	1,195	
	United Arab Emirates	2,276	
	Yemen Arab Republic	445	
	Yemen, People's Democratic Rep. of	865	
		23,414	3.62
R.N. Malhotra (India)	Bangladesh	2,530	
A.S. Jayawardena	Bhutan	267	
(Sri Lanka)	India	17,425	
	Sri Lanka	2,035	
		22,257	3.44

Director *Alternate*	Casting Votes of	Votes by Country and Con- stituency[1]	Percent of Fund Total[2]
ELECTED (continued)			
John Tvedt (Norway)	Denmark	4,900	
Arne Lindå	Finland	4,180	
(Sweden)	Iceland	685	
	Norway	4,675	
	Sweden	7,000	
		21,440	3.31
N'Faly Sangare (Guinea)	Botswana	385	
E.I.M. Mtei	Burundi	595	
(Tanzania)	Ethiopia	790	
	The Gambia	385	
	Guinea	700	
	Kenya	1,285	
	Lesotho	355	
	Liberia	805	
	Malawi	535	
	Nigeria	5,650	
	Sierra Leone	715	
	Sudan	1,570	
	Swaziland	430	
	Tanzania	1,075	
	Uganda	1,000	
	Zambia	2,365	
	Zimbabwe	1,750	
		20,390	3.15
A. Hasnan Habib	Burma	1,345	
(Indonesia)	Fiji	520	
Jaafar Ahmad	Indonesia	7,450	
(Malaysia)	Lao People's Dem. Rep.	490	
	Malaysia	4,045	
	Nepal	535	
	Singapore	1,174	
	Thailand	2,965	
	Viet Nam	1,600	
		20,124	3.11

Director *Alternate*	Casting Votes of	Votes by Country and Con- stituency[1]	Percent of Fund Total[2]
ELECTED (continued)			
Alexandre Kafka (Brazil)	Brazil	10,225	
César Robalino	Colombia	3,145	
(Ecuador)	Dominican Republic	1,075	
	Ecuador	1,300	
	Guyana	625	
	Haiti	595	
	Panama	925	
	Suriname	625	
	Trinidad and Tobago	1,480	
		19,995	3.09
ZHANG Zicun	China	18,250	2.82
(CHANG Tse Chun)			
(China)			
WANG Enshao (China)			
Ghassem Salehkhou	Afghanistan	925	
(Islamic Republic of Iran)	Algeria	4,525	
Omar Kabbaj (Morocco)	Ghana	1,840	
	Iran, Islamic Republic of	6,850	
	Morocco	2,500	
	Tunisia	1,195	
		17,835	2.76
Alvaro Donoso (Chile)	Argentina	8,275	
Mario Teijeiro	Bolivia	925	
(Argentina)	Chile	3,505	
	Paraguay	595	
	Peru	2,710	
	Uruguay	1,510	
		17,520	2.71

Director *Alternate*	Casting Votes of	Votes by Country and Con- stituency[1]	Percent of Fund Total[2]
ELECTED (concluded)			
Abderrahmane Alfidja	Benin	490	
(Niger)	Cameroon	925	
wa Bilenga Tshishimbi	Cape Verde	280	
(Zaïre)	Central African		
	Republic	490	
	Chad	490	
	Comoros	285	
	Congo	505	
	Djibouti	307	
	Equatorial Guinea	400	
	Gabon	700	
	Guinea-Bissau	309	
	Ivory Coast	1,390	
	Madagascar	760	
	Mali	655	
	Mauritania	505	
	Mauritius	655	
	Niger	490	
	Rwanda	595	
	São Tomé and Principe	280	
	Senegal	880	
	Togo	535	
	Upper Volta	490	
	Zaïre	2,530	
		14,946	2.31
Total		636,318	98.33

[1]Voting power varies on certain matters pertaining to the General Department with use of the Fund's resources in that Department.

[2]This total does not include the votes of Egypt, Democratic Kampuchea, and South Africa, which did not participate in the 1982 Regular Election of Executive Directors. The combined votes of those members total 10,780, or 1.67 percent of those in the General Department and Special Drawing Rights Department.

Summary of Discussion

The discussion focused on the influence of the developing countries on decision making in the Fund, on the need for, and possible effects of, an increase in the share of these countries in the total voting power of the Fund, and the prospects for the Fund's becoming the world's central bank.

In October 1982, the developing countries accounted for about 40 percent of voting power in the Fund; excluding the oil exporting countries, the share was about 30 percent. Decisions taken by the Fund's governing bodies—the Board of Governors and the Executive Board—were subject to different majorities, but the minimum was 50 percent. Therefore, even if the developing countries were fully united, they would not have sufficient voting power to determine decisions taken in these bodies. Participants argued that, because the developing countries constituted 86 percent of the Fund's membership (77 percent for the non-oil developing countries), equity called for a considerable increase in their voting power. They noted that, in the United Nations, the smallest developing country had one vote, the same as the largest industrial country.

The Fund staff replied that the influence of the developing countries on the Fund's decision making was probably larger than the share of these countries in total voting power might suggest. The developing countries, like the industrial countries, had veto power over proposals in many important areas. Some decisions in the Fund, such as decisions on membership, required the support of 85 percent of total voting power; others, such as decisions on charges for the use of Fund resources, required a 70 percent majority. The developing countries, when voting together, could block proposals subject to these majorities. It was noted that the 70 percent figure had been selected with the voting share of developing countries in mind. The developing countries also benefited from both the manner in which decisions were taken by the Executive Board and the composition of that Board. Most issues considered by the Executive Board were resolved by consensus;

although it was inevitable that the Board's resolutions strongly reflected the distribution of voting power, this procedure allowed individual Executive Directors to influence the Board's discussions by their arguments. The practice of decision making by consensus tended to favor the developing countries, which elected half of the Fund's 22 Executive Directors and which formed part of the constituencies of some Executive Directors elected mainly by industrial countries.

The Fund staff also suggested that a redistribution of voting power from the industrial to the developing countries would not necessarily further the interests of the developing countries. They noted that, when the creation of the International Monetary Fund was being considered during the period leading up to the Bretton Woods Conference in July 1944, it was decided that both subscriptions and voting power should reflect the relative economic importance of the countries that would be members of the organizations. One of the purposes of this decision was to assure the countries that provided the Fund with the bulk of its resources that they would have a major influence on the policies and practices affecting the use of these resources. If the voting power of the developing countries were to be increased by weakening the link between voting power and quotas, the industrial countries might become less willing to provide the Fund with the resources it needed to make loans on reasonable terms to its members, including developing country members. If, on the other hand, the voting power of developing countries were to be increased by raising the share of these countries in total quotas, the ratio of the Fund's usable resources to its total resources would decline, again impairing the organization's ability to lend to its members. There was a danger, therefore, that redistribution of voting power from the industrial countries to the developing countries, and thus from countries that supplied the Fund with most of its usable resources to countries that needed to borrow these resources, might reduce the total volume of resources available to the Fund.

Participants were interested in the question of whether the Fund could become the world's central bank. The Fund staff suggested that there could only be a limited parallel between a national central bank and the Fund. A basic similarity was that, historically, central banks emerged as a result of the perceived need for a national institution to conduct monetary policy and of the political will to endow an institution with the requisite powers. Similarly, at the international level, the experience of the 1930s demonstrated that an institution to promote international monetary cooperation would be sorely needed in the postwar era, and the creation of the Fund was a conscious political act to meet that need. Also, as in the case of many central banks, the purposes of the Fund included the promotion and maintenance of high levels of employment and real income. The purposes of the Fund, however, also included the promotion of balanced international trade and orderly exchange arrangements among its members, and the amelioration of maladjustments in its members' balance of payments. In respect of these purposes and the corresponding functions of the Fund, there could be no parallel because, unlike a central bank, the Fund was an organization of sovereign countries.

The authority that the Fund had to create special drawing rights had only a very limited similarity to the monopoly power of a central bank over the national money supply. Moreover, the Fund did not have activities comparable to, say, the rediscount window or the open market operations of a central bank. The financial resources made available by the Fund to its members were normally in support of adjustment programs designed to correct balance of payments disequilibria, and the Fund's relationship with its member countries was fundamentally different from that of a central bank with its customers. Thus, there existed a limited parallel between the purposes and activities of the Fund and those of a central bank. But the Fund, as an organization of sovereign member countries, had and would continue to have several functions that were unique to it. Possible evolution of the Fund toward becoming the central bank of the world would seem to be closely related to the willingness of member countries to transfer their monetary and economic sovereignty to the Fund. It would have to be a political evolution shaped by international monetary developments.

The Current World Economic Situation and the Problem of Global Payments Imbalances

Wm. C. Hood

This paper deals with the economic situation in the world. It is divided in three main sections: (1) problems, (2) policies, and (3) prospects. The paper concludes with a short statement on the role of the Fund in helping to deal with the economic situation.

The subject matter of this paper may be of interest to China for many reasons. International trade, as well as the cost of foreign capital, is of growing importance to China. The prospects for peace in the world depend significantly on economic conditions.

This paper derives its analysis from Fund staff reports to the Executive Board and from the Fund annual publication entitled *World Economic Outlook*.[1] In this paper, major groups of countries rather than individual countries will be referred to. These are the groups commonly referred to in Fund analyses. They are the 21 industrial countries, the 12 major oil exporting countries, and the non-oil developing countries that comprise the 113 other members of the Fund, including China.

Problems

Three major economic problems confront the world. The first is the high rate of inflation; the second is the low rate of growth of output and employment; and the third is the large size of the imbalances in countries' international payments.

---

[1] An updated analysis of developments covered in this paper will be available in the *World Economic Outlook* to be issued in May 1983.

Inflation

The rate of inflation in the world is high, pervasive, persistent, and uneven. It is high in the sense that it is currently more than twice the level of the 1960s and early 1970s. For example, the rate of consumer price inflation in industrial countries in 1981 was 10 percent, compared with an average of about 4 percent per annum during 1963–72. The rate has been decreasing this year and may average slightly more than 8 percent in 1982.

The rate of inflation is pervasive because the current high rate extends to all country groups. Specifically, this year the figure will be more than 11 percent in the oil exporting countries and more than 31 percent in the non-oil developing countries.

The rate of inflation is also persistent because it has remained above 7 percent in the industrial world and above 10 percent in the developing world since 1973.

It is uneven, however, because it varies from country to country. Among the industrial countries, rates as low as 5–6 percent were experienced in the Federal Republic of Germany and Japan in 1981, and among the non-oil developing countries, rates varied from an average of 62 percent for the major exporters of manufactures to an average of 10 percent for the low-income countries in 1981.

The current rates of inflation are a problem for the world economy for several reasons. First, inflation slows down economic growth. This is partly because it adds to uncertainty and therefore makes government and business less willing to undertake the major capital investments that contribute to growth and productivity. Inflation slows down growth also because it leads all sectors in the economy to seek greater economic security through higher nominal incomes and through investment of wealth in protected rather than productive assets. Moreover, as inflation destroys competitiveness, it stifles trade. Second, inflation disrupts international economic relations. Disparities in inflation rates create disparities in interest rates. These latter disparities disturb and distort international capital flows. All of these effects on trade and capital flows generate exchange rate changes, often of a volatile kind, that are difficult for traders to interpret and therefore inhibit international commerce. Third, inflation tends to make richer countries less willing to extend aid and concessional loans to poorer countries just when slower growth and disturbed exchange conditions are making it more difficult for poorer countries to export.

Output and employment

The second major problem of the world economy—low rates of growth of output and employment—derives in considerable part from inflation and also from the effects of demand restraint policies in the industrial countries to reduce inflation. The decline in growth rates has been substantial. In the 14 industrial countries, real gross national product growth in 1980 and 1981 was only about 1 percent, compared with slightly less than 5 percent per annum on average in 1963–72. In 1982, the figure will be virtually zero. It was negative in 3 of the 7 major industrial countries in 1981 and will be negative again in some of them in 1982.

It is more difficult to assess the recent growth performance of the non-oil developing countries because of the wide diversity of experience among them. But after averaging 6 percent per annum during 1968–72, the rate declined to 2¾ percent in 1981, and in 1982, it may be even less than that. Among the major exporters of manufactures, the decline in output growth was from an average of 8 percent in 1968–72 to less than ½ of 1 percent in 1981.

The oil exporting countries experienced a marked reversal in real growth during 1980 and 1981. This was due primarily to reduced oil exports resulting from the strong and sustained response of consumers to the steep rise in oil prices from 1978 to 1980, as well as from the current recession in industrial countries.

The slow growth and associated high unemployment rates of the past two years have imposed heavy economic and social costs on the residents of industrial countries. But their problems have created great difficulties for the developing countries. It has been estimated that each 1 percent decline in economic activity in the industrial countries is associated with about a 1.3 percent decline in the volume of exports of the non-oil developing countries. In addition, slow growth in industrial countries typically weakens developing country export prices. It also leads to greater pressure in industrial countries for protection against imports. These two factors compound the effects of slow growth in industrial countries on developing country export earnings. During 1973–80, non-oil developing countries exhibited a certain resiliency against the impact of slower growth in industrial countries. These developing countries were able to increase their share of industrial country imports, and they were able to concentrate their exports to some degree on the faster-growing markets. But, as indicated by the lower growth figures for 1981, such opportunities are limited.

An average annual growth rate of 2.5 percent in a group of countries in which the average population growth is proceeding at approximately the same rate implies no real increase in the average standard of living for these countries as a group but does indicate a drastic decrease in the standard of living of some of these countries.

Payments imbalances

The third major problem of the world economy is the large size of the imbalances in countries' international payments.

Before discussing this problem, it must be mentioned that statistics for the balances of payments of countries of the world show some inconsistencies that have become worse in the last couple of years. Conceptually, the sum of the current account positions of all countries must be zero. In practice, because of inadequacies of national statistics, the actual figures do not add to zero. The asymmetry—surpluses too small or deficits too large—has grown considerably. The figure for 1982 is some US$70 billion according to Fund estimates. The Fund staff, like that of other international and national institutions, is naturally concerned about this asymmetry and has attempted to identify its sources. Although its study is incomplete, the Fund staff has found that the problem is concentrated in the categories of flows of services and private transfers rather than merchandise trade, and it is probably attributable to errors and inconsistencies in the accounts of industrial and oil exporting countries (where transfers and services loom large and have increased rapidly during the past few years).

Major swings in current account positions (measured in terms of the balance on goods, services, and private transfers) have been associated with the changes in the price of oil. After the first oil price increases in 1973 and 1974, the surplus of the oil exporting countries rose about tenfold to some US$70 billion, the industrial countries swung from surplus into deficit (about US$14 billion), and the deficit of the non-oil developing countries more than trebled (to US$37 billion). By 1978, the surplus of the oil exporting countries had all but disappeared, the industrial countries had developed a surplus of about US$30 billion, and the non-oil developing countries continued to have a deficit of about the same size (US$39 billion) as in 1974 in nominal terms—though, of course, a much smaller one in real terms. In 1980, the new oil price increases of 1979 and 1980 led to an enormous surplus (US$115 billion) for the oil exporting countries, a renewed deficit (US$45 billion) for the industrial countries, and more than a doubling of the deficit (to US$86 billion) of the non-oil developing countries. In 1981, the industrial countries' deficit virtually disappeared, and the surplus of the oil exporting countries fell dramatically (to less than US$70 billion), but the deficit of the non-oil developing countries continued to increase, to about US$100 billion.

The problem with these imbalances is their sustainability. It is normal for countries with fairly high productivity of additional investment to draw savings from the rest of the world and to record a deficit on current account and a surplus on capital account. As long as the funds thus imported are applied so as to increase income and thus permit servicing of the debts incurred, the payments situation may be described as sustainable. But legitimate questions may be raised as to the sustainability of the 1981 rates of capital inflow to some of the smaller industrial countries and to some of the non-oil developing countries. The debt servicing requirements in some of these countries have risen substantially during the 1970s and may have reached levels that the countries themselves or their creditors feel should not be exceeded. This is a major problem in the world economy at this time. Countries that must reduce their inflow of capital from capital markets have only limited alternatives. They may hope for increased grants or concessional loans, but the prospects for increases in these flows are not bright. Such countries may hope to increase their exports, but because of the slow growth of export markets, these prospects are not good either. Indeed, the volume of world trade did not increase at all in 1981. The only other alternative is to reduce imports. Because of the importance of imports in the production processes of the deficit economies, this form of adjustment frequently means lower output and employment rather than the substitution of domestically produced goods for imports.

Policies

The three main problems of the international economy are related. Inflation impairs growth; impaired growth inhibits adjustment of payments balances. In a sense, therefore, inflation is at the root of the problem. As such, reducing inflation should command priority in the setting of policies. Of course, the same policy prescription is not appropriate for all countries. In this paper, it is not possible to discuss the issues of policy in particular countries. Attention will be given, however, to the policy problems as they occur in groups of countries.

Industrial countries

Because of their great weight in international trade and therefore in the performance of the entire world economy, the policies of the industrial countries, particularly the larger ones, are of special importance. In these countries, priority has been given for many years to the reduction of inflation. The sources of inflation include the overly ambitious demands of social and other policies on the economy, excessive cost increases combined with declining productivity growth, careless monetary policy, and intermittent surges in the prices of food and energy. Whatever the causes of the inflation, its intensity and persistence during an extended period have led to deep-seated expectations that it will continue. These perverse expectations have been nourished by repeated reversals of policy, and they now make the reduction of inflation very difficult.

The main instrument of policy that is used against inflation in the major industrial countries is control over the rate of growth of money. It is widely agreed that the control of monetary growth is absolutely necessary to reduce inflation. But it is also widely recognized that steeply rising fiscal deficits can lead to the loss of monetary control or to the expectation of such a loss and, in this way, inhibit progress toward lower rates of inflation. Nevertheless, in many industrial countries, fiscal policy has not adequately supported monetary policy. Similarly, it is recognized that increases in incomes that are greatly in excess of productivity growth lead to rises in costs that must be reflected in prices if enterprises are to survive. It has proved very difficult, however, in the industrial countries to implement and sustain incomes policies that, together with fiscal discipline, give adequate support to monetary policy.

The excessive reliance on monetary policy has tended to produce interest rates considerably higher than the rate of inflation, particularly in some of the industrial countries. These high interest rates have tended to slow economic growth to a degree greater than might otherwise have been necessary. These two results—higher interest rates and lower growth than necessary to avert inflation—have created special problems for other countries, especially the smaller industrial countries and the developing countries. Beyond these broad aspects of policy in industrial countries, it must be noted that more technical features of the application of policy have resulted in an unwelcome volatility of interest rates and exchange rates. The Fund's approach to policy for the industrial countries has been to emphasize not only the essential role of control of the money supply but also the supportive roles of other policies. The Fund has stressed the importance of adequate fiscal restraint. The Fund has recognized the difficulty of achieving good results through application of incomes policies; but it has noted that such policies, particularly of the flexible or informal type to restrain the growth of incomes, have in some countries served as useful adjuncts to fiscal and monetary policies. Finally, the Fund has encouraged the mature economies of the industrial world to undertake the structural adaptations that are necessary in the face of changing technology and changing relative scarcities. In particular, it has fully supported efforts to conserve the use of energy and to develop sources of energy other than petroleum and has welcomed the considerable success of these efforts.

Non-oil developing countries

The non-oil developing countries display a great variety of situations, and only a few valid generalizations can be made about policies required in them. They are, however, afflicted by the same three economic problems that are troubling the world in general. In many of these countries, these problems are more acute than in the industrial countries, especially the problem of deficits in the current account of international payments. Although improvement of performance by the industrial countries in respect of inflation and output would greatly assist the developing countries, there remains a wide scope for the exercise of policy initiatives by the developing countries themselves.

The management of domestic demand has very often been inadequate because of a tendency to allow fiscal deficits to become excessive. A variety of factors contribute to this result, with different ones being more important in some countries than in others. These factors include excessive spending on social capital or social programs, inadequate control over public sector wages, budget support of uncompetitive industries, subsidizing of key commodities, faulty tax administration, shrinkage of tax bases, and unwillingness to increase tax rates when needed to reduce deficits. In many developing countries, because of the limitations of the domestic capital market, there is little scope for domestic financing of fiscal deficits other than through an increase in central bank monetary liabilities. Accordingly, an overly large fiscal deficit is usually accompanied by a monetary expansion greater than is warranted in existing conditions of inflation.

In some instances, the situation might improve if interest rates were allowed to rise. Higher rates would probably have only a limited effect on the amount of savings. Nevertheless, they would be more likely to induce savings flows into financial institutions, as opposed to inflation hedges, and through such institutions into productive investments. On the whole, real interest rates have tended to be positive in those developing countries that are major exporters of manufactured goods. Limited flexibility of interest rates has tended to curb the effectiveness of policy, especially in the primary producing countries.

Exchange rate policy has also inhibited improvement of performance in certain countries. On the whole, those countries that followed a flexible exchange rate policy were more successful in keeping their prices in line with world prices, and thereby retaining competitiveness, than those countries that did not allow their exchange rates to reflect relative inflation rates. If exchange rate changes are to exert their full impact on the economy, they must be accompanied by supportive monetary and fiscal policies as well as measures pertaining to performance in specific sectors or industries.

There have also been instances in which policies of financial management have not been appropriate. It has been essential for most non-oil developing countries to increase their import of capital during the difficult years of adjustment to the many consequences of the rapid increases in oil and other prices. These countries have had to determine the sustainable level of the capital inflow. The judgment they have made has not always been wise, and when mistakes have occurred they have usually been in the direction of permitting too large a capital inflow. This has resulted in the piling up of payments arrears, debt rescheduling, and a general reduction in creditworthiness of the country in question as judged in the world capital markets. This is not to deny that there have been circumstances in which quite unpredictable events have unfortunately placed countries in positions that required debt rescheduling.

The Fund's approach to the policy problems of developing countries has two features. The first feature concerns the policy actions that may be taken by the developing countries themselves. The second feature concerns the help that wise policy in the industrial countries can render.

The Fund has urged developing countries to maintain control over fiscal deficits in order to avoid the excessive monetary expansion that may be induced through the financing of these deficits. Although the Fund does not express specific views to governments concerning the allocation of expenditure or the sources of their revenues, the Fund has advised against unduly large wage increases in the public sector and against widespread or extensive programs for subsidizing the costs of basic commodities or public services. In addition, the Fund has urged countries to avoid negative real interest rates and to encourage savings and the development of financial institutions and markets. The Fund also seeks to judge the appropriateness of its members' exchange rates and to make its views on this matter known to the authorities of the country concerned. The Fund also offers advice on the policies that might usefully accompany or support any change in a member's exchange rate.

In respect of the help that industrial countries can render to the developing countries, the Fund has stressed the following points. It has urged the view that slow growth in the developed world greatly damages developing countries. It has also noted the very serious impact of high interest rates on the deficits of the developing countries. The Fund has urged the developed countries to keep their markets open. In particular, it has repeatedly stressed the importance of avoiding protection or restrictions against imports of goods and services. Equally, it has pointed to the need to keep capital markets open for the appropriate use of developing countries. Finally, it has urged the industrial countries, especially in the recent period, to maintain the flows of aid and concessional finance to the poorest countries. These countries have little access to capital markets and have virtually no capacity to adjust payments imbalances other than by reducing their standards of living.

Prospects

1983

Before commenting on the outlook for 1983, it would be well to recall the three major assumptions on which the projections are based. First, current economic policies will apply through 1983. Second, the exchange rates prevailing in mid-June 1982 will prevail through 1983. Third, the average price of oil will remain constant in nominal terms in the second half of 1982 and will remain constant through 1983 in real terms (as defined by the prices paid for their imports by the oil exporting countries). It should be noted that the projections described here were those available in the Fund in mid-July 1982.

Turning first to the problem of inflation, it can be reported that some progress is being made. The overall rate of inflation in the industrial countries, as measured by the gross domestic product (GDP) deflator, peaked in 1980 at 9 percent. For 1982, it probably will be some 1½ percentage points below the peak and will drop further in 1983, perhaps by as much as ½ or 1 percentage point.

In the non-oil developing countries, as measured by the consumer price index, the peak of inflation was also reached in 1980 at about 32 percent. By 1982, the average will have dropped slightly. The net oil exporters[2] are still experiencing increases in their inflation rates on average. The inflation rate of the net oil importers among the non-oil developing countries has probably dropped by about 3 percentage points between 1980 and 1982. Some further drop in inflation rates in 1983 is expected among both the net oil exporters and the net oil importers.

As noted above, in 1982 there has been virtually no growth of output, on average, in the industrial world. In the United States, the figure is likely to decrease by more than 1 percent. For 1983, some revival in the growth of output is expected for the industrial countries; the rate might reach 2½ percent.

---

[2] These are countries, other than the main oil exporting countries, whose oil exports exceeded their oil imports in most of the 1970s.

Growth among the oil exporting countries has been declining in each of the last three years, owing principally to the reduced demand for oil. This year, the decline—at some 2.5 percent—will be less than the decline of 4.5 percent experienced in 1981. The expectation for 1983 is that, with a revival of world demand for oil, real growth in these countries may increase by some 7 percent.

The non-oil developing countries, which grew at a rate of some 2.8 percent in 1981, are growing at a rate of 2.5 percent in 1982. In 1983, the expectation is that their growth performance will have improved to a rate of 4 percent, in line with the expected modest revival of economic activity in the industrial world.

Turning now to the current account of the balance of payments, the oil exporting countries had a surplus of some US$70 billion in 1981. Owing to a further projected decline in the volume of oil exports and a further projected decline in their terms of trade, the current account surplus is expected to decline to about US$15 billion in 1982. In 1983, the pickup in the world demand for oil will lead to an increase in the overall current account surplus of the oil exporting countries to perhaps US$25 billion.

For the industrial countries, the combination of a soft world oil market and continued slow growth should transform the 1981 deficit of US$4 billion into a surplus of US$8 billion in 1982. While the surplus of the industrial countries is forecast to grow to perhaps US$13 billion in 1983, the movements within the industrial countries will be disparate. The United States has increased its surplus somewhat in 1982, but it is expected to have virtually no surplus in 1983, as its oil imports rise and more particularly as the recent appreciation of the dollar begins to show its effects on trade. The Federal Republic of Germany and Japan are in the process of a major increase of surplus positions in 1982–83. The United Kingdom, on the other hand, is experiencing a considerable decline in its surplus during 1982 and 1983. The industrial countries, other than the United States, Japan, the Federal Republic of Germany, and the United Kingdom, recorded a combined deficit of some US$36 billion in 1981. This deficit is expected to be lower in 1982 and in 1983. Indeed, in 1983 it may be only about half as large as in 1981.

The combined current account deficit of the non-oil developing countries, which was about US$100 billion in 1981, is expected to fall in both 1982 and 1983, reaching US$90 billion in 1983. Expressed in real terms, for example, as a percentage of the value of exports, the projected deficit in 1982 and 1983 will be at a level corresponding to the average of the late 1960s and early 1970s and will be below the level of the peak deficits of 1974–75 and 1980–81. The projected decline in the real current account deficit occurs exclusively in those non-oil developing countries that are net importers of oil and, within that group, primarily in the larger countries having considerable flexibility in their external transactions. Two principal "plus factors" that help to reduce the real deficit are the stabilization of oil prices and the reduction in inflation in industrial countries. Both of these factors moderate the growth in the costs of imports in non-oil developing countries. Adjustment policies that help to reduce the growth of imports in terms of volume also reduce the real deficit in these countries. Among the "minus factors" that limit the improvement in the real deficit are the continued slow growth in industrial countries and the rising costs of servicing the accumulating debt of the non-oil developing countries.

In summary, inflation rates are now generally moving in the right direction, and rates of output, though still low, are rising—albeit somewhat uncertainly. But the structure of payments is still unsatisfactory, particularly with respect to many smaller industrial countries and non-oil developing countries. The sustainability of the deficits of many countries in these categories is highly questionable. Adjustment of their positions either through improvement of their export growth or curtailment of imports must be contemplated in the medium term.

The medium term

In its consideration of medium-term prospects, the Fund staff has developed alternative scenarios. These scenarios are elaborated in the *World Economic Outlook* published in April 1982. Their general character and implications are summarized here. The purpose of the scenarios is to assess the medium-term implications of alternative policy stances in industrial countries on the industrial world itself and on the performance of the non-oil developing countries.

The central scenario is based on the assumption that industrial countries affected by inflation will persist with policies of monetary restraint and will reinforce those policies with supportive fiscal policies and policies to reduce structural rigidities in goods and labor markets. A more pessimistic scenario is also elaborated in which fiscal and monetary policies are not combined harmoniously to reduce inflation, either because of an untimely relaxation of monetary policy or because of inadequate fiscal support for the monetary policy.

In the central scenario, economic growth in the industrial countries would average slightly more than 3 percent per annum during 1984–86. This improvement over projected rates for 1982–83 would not be sufficient to reduce unemployment significantly below current levels. An improvement in the rate of inflation (as measured by GDP deflators) to about 5–5½ percent by 1986 is also projected in this scenario. The more pessimistic scenario contains a projected annual growth rate of only about 2 percent in 1984–86 and a rate of inflation of some 8½ percent.

In elaborating the implications of these alternative scenarios for the non-oil developing countries, a number of assumptions were made. It must be remembered that the results of the analysis depend explicitly on these assumptions. With respect to policies, a crucial assumption is that the developing countries that are confronted with serious external imbalances will implement comprehensive programs of adjustment, programs that are more severe according to the more pessimistic scenarios than according to the more moderate central scenario. In addition, it is assumed that real interest rates in international markets will be reduced to about 2 percent by 1986, that oil prices will remain constant in real terms at their 1983 levels, that the trade protectionism of the industrial countries against the exports of the non-oil developing countries will not change, and that official development assistance will be maintained in real terms from 1981 through 1986.

In the central scenario, growth rates would be higher in the non-oil developing countries in 1984–86 than in 1982. This increase would vary among the different groups of countries.

The non-oil developing countries as a group would show a lower ratio of current account deficit to exports in 1986 than in 1982 in the central scenario. In the more pessimistic scenario, however, there would be virtually no change.

The improvement of the current account position according to the central scenario is particularly marked for the net oil exporters and for the major exporters of manufactures. The low-income group of developing countries (excluding India and the People's Republic of

China), which has the highest deficit/export ratio, would experience some reduction in this ratio between 1982 and 1986, but it would still remain substantially above its 1972 level. This group's debt service ratio would show a similar pattern of movement. The other developing countries, consisting mainly of middle-income countries exporting chiefly primary products, would experience reductions in their deficit/ exports and deficit/debt service ratios, but both ratios would remain above 1972 levels. Both India and the People's Republic of China are expected to maintain relatively low levels of external debt. India's current account deficit is projected to decline significantly up to 1986 in the central scenario. China's current account deficit is expected to remain moderate.

The results for the central scenario envisage a very considerable adjustment effort on the part of the non-oil developing countries. This effort would be greatly assisted by the modest resumption of growth and the lower interest rates in the industrial world. It is the Fund's judgment that the payments deficits envisaged according to these scenarios are capable of being financed. This is not to imply that the financial system may not be under some strain. On the contrary, if many difficult debt reschedulings are required or if negotiations of some reschedulings break down and confidence in the banking or financial system is affected, the system will be under considerable strain.

The much less favorable results according to the more pessimistic scenario raise more serious questions as to whether the deficits envisaged under that scenario could be financed in the circumstances.

The analysis embodied in the scenarios emphasizes the very great need to implement and maintain policies of adjustment that will reduce inflation throughout the world economy, permit resumption of growth, and establish a structure of viable payments positions.

The Role of the Fund

The Fund's critical and unique role is in helping countries to design and implement appropriate adjustment programs. In the design of such programs, the aim is to reduce current account deficits to a level that can be serviced out of a growing income. Sound fiscal and monetary policies are central to an adjustment program, but complementary measures to improve economic efficiency and to extend a country's productive base are usually also called for. Commercial financial institutions are, and will continue to be, the principal source of balance of payments financing. But in the light of balance of payments disturbances of recent years, the Fund has increased its capacity to support appropriate adjustment programs. It has also increased members' access to its resources relative to their quotas and has extended the period during which resources may be used in circumstances requiring structural adjustments in a member's economy.

The Fund maintains a surveillance over exchange rates and exchange rate policies of members. A very important aspect of this function of surveillance is to point out to members how these policies inhibit or facilitate the adjustments that other members need to make. This effort to promote the mutual consistency of policies is concerned with the effects of industrial countries' policies on developing countries as well as with the interactions of industrial countries among themselves. It is the Fund's purpose to promote a viable structure of payments and associated exchange rates in the world as a whole.

Related Reading

Goldstein, Morris, and Mohsin S. Khan, *Effects of Slowdown in Industrial Countries on Growth in Non-Oil Developing Countries,* IMF Occasional Paper No. 12 (Washington, August 1982).

International Monetary Fund, *World Economic Outlook: A Survey by the Staff of the International Monetary Fund,* IMF Occasional Paper No. 9 (Washington, April 1982).

Summary of Discussion

The discussion focused on inflation: its causes, its effects on growth and employment, and policies to combat it. Inflation in the industrial countries was emphasized, although the possible transmission of inflation from the industrial to the developing countries was also discussed.

The rise in inflation in the industrial countries from the mid-1960s through the 1970s was attributed to a variety of causes. Several participants cited policies adopted in these countries, including overly expansionary fiscal and monetary policies, and structural imbalances affecting the patterns of expenditure, output, and incomes. Reference was also made to the possibility that the emergence of high inflation and its coexistence with high unemployment could be due to fundamental weaknesses in the market-oriented economies of Western countries.

The Fund staff agreed that expansionary fiscal policies accompanied by relatively loose monetary policies had been a major cause of the high inflation in the industrial countries. They noted that the ratio of budget expenditure and budget deficit to gross national product (GNP) had risen appreciably in most of these countries and that this rise was associated in part with growing expenditure on social security and other entitlement programs. Other contributing factors included the rise in grain prices in the early 1970s resulting from widespread crop failures and the increases in oil prices in 1973–74 and 1978–79.

The Fund staff attributed the intractability of inflation to strong expectations, especially among trade unions and enterprises, of continued large price increases. Once unions started to expect, partly because of their recent experience, that inflation would remain high during the periods covered by upcoming wage contracts, they began to demand wage increases that would protect the real income of their members from the effects of this anticipated inflation. Enterprises, which had formed similar expectations for largely the same reasons, were willing to meet these wage demands, as long as they felt they could pass on the increased costs in higher prices. But, in due time, these higher costs and the higher interest rates associated with inflation discouraged capital spending. This effect, combined with poorer export sales, the inability of consumers to maintain spending in real terms, and official policy constraints on spending, eventually led to unemployment and excess capacity. Lately, these effects had in their turn begun to moderate inflationary expectations, and the year-to-year rise in consumer prices in the industrial countries as a group declined from slightly more than 12 percent in March 1980 to about 7 percent in September 1982.

The participants showed considerable interest in the effects of lending through the Euromarkets on world inflation. It was suggested that the effects might be positive, since the Euromarkets would facilitate the transmission of inflationary impulses from countries that were net lenders in the markets, including many industrial countries, to countries that were net borrowers, most of which were developing countries. It was also suggested that the inflationary effects might be quite large, since outstanding loans made through the Euromarkets were more than US$2,000 billion, or about one sixth of world GNP. The Fund staff argued that the Euromarkets did not initiate inflation, but they agreed that they might provide a channel for its transfer from one country to another. They cautioned, however, against exaggerating the importance of such transfers, noting that about two thirds of outstanding claims in the market were interbank and that the expansion of nonbank claims relative to the total demand of countries that borrowed in the markets had not been unduly large.

Participants also discussed the possible beneficial effects associated with inflation. It was argued that expansionary fiscal and monetary policies that gave rise to inflation might, at the same time, provide a boost to growth and employment. It was also suggested that, by reducing the real cost of borrowing, inflation directly encouraged investment, again contributing to higher growth and employment. However, other participants, including the Fund staff, claimed that any such beneficial effects would be short-lived because of the adverse effects of inflation on wage costs, on the confidence attached to estimates of returns to investment, and on the pattern of resource allocation.

The discussion of policies to combat inflation centered on the effectiveness of specific policies and on the importance of the policy mix. Some participants believed that the experience of the industrial countries during the 1970s demonstrated the inability of supply-side and monetary policies to achieve reasonable stability of prices. Others argued that both sets of policies had important contributions to make. Supply-side policies directed at providing appropriate incentives fostered increased supplies of labor and savings, as well as more efficient patterns of investment and production, and thus contributed to the moderation of inflation by increasing the supply of goods and services. Policies aimed at restricting the supply and/or increasing the cost of money tackled inflation by containing the growth of aggregate demand for goods and services. The decline in inflation in the United States in the last few years could be attributed largely to the tight money policy introduced in 1979.

Nevertheless, there was widespread agreement that neither supply-side policies nor monetary policies should be relied on exclusively to combat inflation. What was needed, the Fund staff suggested, was a mix of policies aimed at increasing supply through the provision of adequate incentives, restricting the growth of aggregate demand through fiscal as well as monetary policies, and restraining wage and profit claims through incomes policies. With respect to the last, incomes policies that were implemented through edicts would probably not be effective, but those based on a cooperative approach among representatives of government, unions, and enterprises could play an important complementary role in combating inflation.

The importance of the fiscal-monetary policy mix was also emphasized. It was noted that, in order to dampen inflationary expectations, it was essential that both the fiscal situation and the rate of monetary expansion be well controlled, both in fact and in the eyes of the community. Doubts as to the willingness of the authorities to firmly manage one of these policies could reduce the effectiveness of the other policy.

Some Comments on the Current Economic Situation in the West

Hong Junyan

In the past, economists have often held different views on the global economic situation. Their forecasts with regard to the future course of the world economy have also varied. Some have been optimistic, some have been pessimistic, and some have adopted a wait-and-see attitude. Recently, however, most of the economists in the West have become increasingly pessimistic about the world economic situation and its future. Their anxiety is not uncalled for. In this paper, I will present some of my views on the current economic situation in the West.

Economic Developments in the West and Their Consequences

The current world economic situation is indeed grim. The present downward trend of economic activity in the capitalist world began in 1979–80. Since that time, economic policies adopted in the principal capitalist countries have followed a tortuous and complicated course, which, in turn, has given rise to new situations and created new problems.

The present worldwide economic crisis began with the recession in 1979, and, from April 1979 to July 1980, industrial production in the United States declined by 8.6 percent. Although during August 1980–July 1981 U.S. industrial production rose to its level prior to the crisis, it began to decline again in August 1981. From August 1981 to October 1982, industrial production fell by 11.4 percent, and this downward trend has continued into September 1982. In September 1982, the rate of unemployment reached 10.1 percent, and the number of jobless totaled 11.3 million—a record figure since 1941. At the same time, the utilization of industrial capacity fell to 69.4 percent, the lowest level since 1975. The rate of capacity utilization in the automobile industry was only 55 percent. All other industrial indicators showed similar downward trends—lower investment in fixed capital, decline in new orders for durable goods, slower rate of construction of new housing, and reduction in the volume of retail sales. Following a year of modest recovery beginning in mid-1980, however, recession re-emerged—a situation not experienced in the United States since the end of the Second World War.

The United Kingdom was the first among Western European countries to have been affected by the economic crisis. From July 1979 to May 1981, its industrial production fell by 14.3 percent—a record decline since the War. In the same period, industrial production in the Federal Republic of Germany fell by 9 percent, while that of France declined by 11.1 percent. However, unlike the United States, the Western European countries have experienced neither a tangible recovery nor a second recession. Their economies have been characterized by stagnation and inflation. Some rises have been registered, but these have been neither large nor sustained. Such a situation also is unprecedented for these countries since the War. In September 1982, unemployment in the member countries of the European Community reached 10.1 percent, and the number of unemployed exceeded 11.2 million. Among these countries, the rate of unemployment was 13.8 percent in the United Kingdom, with 3.29 million workers jobless.

Economic developments have been more favorable in Japan than in the other major capitalist countries. Industrial production began to decline in February 1980 and by August had fallen by 6.1 percent. It began to rise again after September, although unevenly, and reached its highest pre-crisis level in June 1981. However, it fell again from November 1981 to March 1982. In 1981, industrial and mining production increased by 4 percent, and the rate of unemployment reached 2 percent. At present, the Japanese economy is characterized by fluctuations, and its growth rate has been low.

Briefly, the current stagflation in the United States, Western Europe, and Japan has developed over a considerable period of time— since the 1970s—and has manifested itself in slow growth of production, high unemployment, and continuing inflation in these countries.

It is particularly important to note that the economic problems encountered by the major capitalist countries have had serious repercussions on the economies of the developing countries. Not only have the prices of primary commodities exported by developing countries fallen, but, at the same time, the costs of capital goods exported by industrial countries have increased and high interest rates have continued to prevail in capital markets. All of these developments have had a most unfavorable impact on the growth prospects of a large number of developing countries, particularly the non-oil developing countries. These countries are faced with ever-increasing problems: with the sharp drop in the prices of their exports, their export income has also fallen. Furthermore, their trade has been seriously hampered by the protectionist measures adopted by some industrial countries.

In 1981, the per capita income of the developing countries declined for the first time since the War. The balance of payments deficit of the non-oil developing countries is projected to be US$100 billion. Because of mounting trade deficits, high interest rates in international money markets, and fluctuating exchange rates of the major currencies, the debt burden of these countries has continued to increase, and they have found it more and more difficult to borrow in international capital markets. According to data compiled by the International Monetary Fund, the foreign debt of developing countries totaled US$540 billion in 1981, US$372 billion of which was owed to commercial banks. It is estimated that the foreign debt of these countries will reach nearly US$640 billion by the end of 1982. Moreover, many developing countries have had to pay as much as 30–40 percent of their export incomes as annual interest payments.

Causes of the Present Economic Crisis

The present economic crisis did not emerge by accident. As an old Chinese saying goes, it takes more than one cold day for the river to freeze three feet deep—the problems had been developing for quite some time. In my view, the present situation is the inevitable outcome of certain weaknesses inherent in the capitalist system—or, in other words, the result of various contradictions of capitalism developing over a long period of time. Therefore, in order to identify the causes, it is necessary to survey the whole course of development of the Western economy after the War. Only with a proper understanding of the economic situation of the past can we understand the present and also forecast what the future holds for us.

The economies of the major capitalist countries grew rapidly in the 1950s and the 1960s. For instance, in the 1960s, the average annual growth rate of industrial production in the United States was 5.5 percent. The corresponding growth rates were 6.3 percent in Canada, 5.4 percent in France, 5.8 percent in the Federal Republic of Germany, 8.0 percent in Italy, 14.8 percent in Japan, and 3.5 percent in the United Kingdom. At that time, most of the economists in the West had a rather optimistic view of the future of the world economy. Some even claimed that a new "vitality" had been injected into the capitalist system and that the capitalist countries could attain "everlasting prosperity." In fact, however, the rapid growth that took place in the West in the 1950s and the 1960s stemmed from certain specific conditions.

First, scientific and technical innovations after the Second World War helped to open up new areas for investment. The growth of new industries, as well as technological improvements in traditional industries, gave a marked impetus to large-scale renewal and expansion of fixed capital, which led to increased production and employment. Because the adoption of advanced technologies greatly accelerated the productivity of labor, real wages, too, continued to grow. As a result, the consumption level also increased.

Second, the availability of low-priced raw materials, particularly cheap petroleum, from Third World countries helped the rapid economic expansion of the major capitalist countries. The prices of primary products had been falling for some time—from 1950 to 1970. At the same time, the prices of industrial goods increased. In the United States, for example, these prices rose at an average annual rate of 2.5 percent during 1950–73. However, petroleum prices were considerably lower at that time. Prior to the rises in 1973–74, the price of crude oil had been set at US$3 a barrel. Thus, the economic prosperity of the Western countries during this period was built on exploiting the cheap raw materials, including oil, provided by the Third World.

Third, an international monetary system centered on the U.S. dollar and an international trade system (under the auspices of the General Agreement on Tariffs and Trade) with the United States at the center were established after the War. They played a major role in stabilizing the international monetary system and ensuring free trade and the free circulation of funds. As a result, favorable conditions were created for the development of international trade after the War. Growth in trade, in turn, promoted economic growth. In the 1960s, exports of the capitalist countries increased at an average annual rate of 8.1 percent —higher than the 5 percent growth rate of their industrial production.

Fourth, after the War, the role of the state was greatly strengthened in the major capitalist countries, and there was increased intervention by the state in the private sector. The governments of the Western countries adopted Keynesian financial measures to stimulate their economies. Whenever there was a recession, government spending was increased, taxes were reduced, and bank rates were lowered so as to boost demand and increase production. On the other hand, when the economies became excessively inflated, administrative expenditures were reduced, taxes were increased, and bank rates were raised to moderate demand. At a time when the Western economies were experiencing high rates of growth, these measures helped to avert crises.

However, in the 1970s, particularly after 1974–75, the economy of the West changed its course of development from high growth to low growth. In the 1970s, the average annual growth rate of industrial production fell to 4.0 percent in Canada, 3.4 percent in France, 2.7 percent in the Federal Republic of Germany, 3.6 percent in Italy, 5.1 percent in Japan, 1.2 percent in the United Kingdom, and 3.2 percent in the United States. The question is why was there a change of such magnitude between the growth rates in the 1970s and the 1960s. As I mentioned earlier, I believe that the shift from favorable to unfavorable conditions for development of the Western economy was caused by an intensification of the contradictory elements inherent in capitalism.

First, for a number of reasons, a surplus in productive capacity developed, and investment in fixed capital began to fall in the 1970s. The spurt in innovations in science and technology that had led to economic growth in an earlier period declined, and problems emerged in both domestic and world markets.

In the United States, for example, new investment in fixed capital increased by an average of 3.1 percent a year in the 1950s, 6.2 percent a year in the 1960s, and 2.6 percent a year in the 1970s. Similar decreases in investment took place in other Western countries during the 1970s. The lower rate of increase in fixed capital also affected the rise of labor productivity.

Second, the 1970s witnessed a new growth in national liberation movements around the world. The struggle for independence in oil in the Third World has hit the Western economy hard. During the first oil crisis in 1973–74, oil prices were raised threefold in a short period, and prices increased again by more than twofold during the second crisis in 1979–80. Along with the oil price rises, prices of other raw materials increased. The united struggle of the developing countries to gain control of their own products has made it impossible for the large capitalist countries to accelerate capital accumulation at the expense of other countries. This has necessarily impeded growth in the Western countries.

Third, the relatively stable environment of the international monetary and trading system with the United States at the center came to an end in the 1970s. In 1971, the United States ended gold convertibility and devalued the dollar for the first time since the War. In 1973, the Bretton Woods system of fixed exchange rates with the U.S. dollar at the center collapsed, and since that time the monetary system of the capitalist world has lost its stability and the main currencies have been floating. This monetary instability has seriously affected the foreign trade of the capitalist countries. According to data from the Organization for Economic Cooperation and Development, these countries' exports increased at an average annual rate of 8.1 percent between 1960 and 1973, whereas between 1974 and 1979 the average was only 4.5 percent.

Fourth, the long-term practice of Keynesianism—stimulating social demand and boosting economic growth by expanding government spending and incurring a budget deficit—only heightens the disparities between production and consumption. The disastrous effect of prolonged budget deficits was keenly felt in the 1970s. Increases in money supply beyond normal circulation needs to cover budget deficits resulted in increasingly serious inflation. Thus, inflation, monopolistic price setting, and oil price increases combined to generate even further inflation. The average annual increases in consumer prices in the 1960s were 2.7 percent in Canada, 4.1 percent in France, 2.6 percent in the Federal Republic of Germany, 4.0 percent in Italy, 5.9 percent in Japan, 4.1 percent in the United Kingdom, and 2.8 percent in the United States. By comparison, in 1979, these increases were 9.2

percent in Canada, 10.5 percent in France, 4.1 percent in the Federal
Republic of Germany, 15.7 percent in Italy, 3.6 percent in Japan,
15.8 percent in the United Kingdom, and 13.3 percent in the United
States. Spiraling inflation has aggravated the instability of the Western
economy and has created a dilemma for the authorities. For instance,
measures to stimulate domestic demand would only aggravate inflation, and measures to control inflation by reducing demand would
only slow down the pace of economic growth and thereby make it even
more difficult to end the crisis. Moreover, inflation produces adverse
effects on a country's standard of living and consequently also affects its
political stability.

Main Characteristics of the Crisis and Future Prospects

As a result of the developments mentioned above, since the mid-
1970s the Western countries have suffered from stagflation—economic
stagnation, high unemployment, and continuing inflation. These
restrict economic growth and interact with one another to form a
vicious circle. The capitalist countries have been unable to rid
themselves of stagflation because too many problems need to be solved
simultaneously. Keynesianism has failed to provide a cure. The new
economic crisis of the capitalist world that developed in 1979–80
emerged against this background of stagflation. Therefore, the new
problems associated with it are closely linked to the fundamental task
of solving the problem of stagflation.

As I mentioned earlier, the combination of recession and uneven
periods of recovery in the current economic crisis is unprecedented in
the postwar era. This phenomenon can be viewed as a manifestation of
a distortion in the business cycle in the context of stagflation. The
major constraint on economic growth is the weakness of demand for
fixed capital investment. It is more profitable to invest in the financial
market than to invest in fixed capital because of the low utilization
ratio of equipment, rising interest rates (resulting from rising prices,
which entail even higher costs), the high cost of investment loans for
entrepreneurs, and economic stagnation and uncertainty with regard to
the future. It is difficult to achieve economic recovery without
adequate investment in capital.

Another new feature of the present crisis is the high rate of unemployment—the highest since the Great Depression of the 1930s. In similar crises in the past, unemployment would increase, although at a slow rate, and would drop to a rather low level when recovery took place. However, there has been a marked change in this respect since the 1970s; now unemployment not only keeps on rising during a crisis but remains at a high level even when the recession is over, a result of protracted stagflation.

A sluggish rate of economic growth leads to fewer job opportunities. A large number of workers have been replaced by modern machinery, and the unemployment problem has been compounded by new entrants to the labor market—youth and women. The combination of unemployment and soaring prices causes purchasing power to shrink, while high interest rates hamper the growth of consumer credit and mortgage loans. And finally, decreasing consumer demand does not lead to economic recovery.

International trade and the international monetary situation have become even more unstable because of stagflation. For the past two years, international trade has stagnated. The market war between the United States, Western Europe, and Japan is intensifying, and protectionism is rapidly gaining ground. The Western countries are finding it more and more difficult to bring about economic recovery by expanding exports. The developing countries, too, are facing great difficulties in their economic development. The international monetary scene is characterized by symptoms of abnormality and instability—drastic fluctuations of exchange rates, sustained high interest rates, abrupt rise and fall of the gold price, and growing international debt.

To free themselves from stagflation, some Western countries are reformulating their economic policies and restructuring their economies. The United States and the United Kingdom, for example, are experimenting with the doctrines of supply-side economics and monetarism, while France is taking measures to enhance nationalization and government intervention in its economy. However, because of the aggravated contradictions inherent in the capitalist economy, these new policies are meeting strong resistance, and it is impossible for the capitalist countries to expect a marked improvement in their economies.

To conclude, it would be extremely difficult for the Western countries to free themselves from stagflation in a short time. Although the current economic crisis has reached or will soon reach its lowest point and a modest economic recovery is expected in the capitalist world by the end of 1982 or in early 1983, stagflation will continue, and no fundamental changes in the capitalist economies can be expected before the end of this decade.

Summary of Discussion

The discussion focused on the prospects for reducing inflation and increasing economic growth in the Western industrial countries, on the effects of the current stagflation in these countries on the balance of payments of developing countries, and on the outlook for economic growth in the developing countries.

Participants agreed that efforts by policymakers to moderate inflation in Western industrial countries had met with limited success during the 1970s. Some suggested, however, that the recent decline in inflation indicated that performance in this area might be much improved in the 1980s. Others cautioned against extrapolating from the recent movements in inflation indices. They argued that the decline in inflation had been due largely to temporary factors, such as reductions in the prices of food and oil, and that these factors could be expected to be reversible. In the United States, the tight monetary policy introduced in 1979 had also played a part in reducing inflation. Doubts were expressed, however, that the monetary restraint could be continued for much longer in the face of mounting concern over the high level of unemployment. It was also noted that the fiscal deficit in the United States was continuing to rise, and it was suggested that this would add to the difficulties of containing inflation.

Participants argued that the prospects for a resumption of strong economic growth and a return to full employment in the Western industrial countries were also bleak. Developments in the 1950s and 1960s had shown that growth could be maintained at a high level for some time in the capitalist economies. However, the good performance during this period had resulted from a special combination of factors that was not likely to recur or be matched in the foreseeable future. Referring to both inflation and unemployment, one participant observed that stagflation in the West was like a moderate but clinging fever—it was not unbearable, but it was difficult to cure.

It was observed that if the growth of gross domestic product were to remain low in the industrial countries, both the increase in volume and the prices of developing country exports to these countries would continue to be low. This would constrain the growth of imports in the developing countries, casting doubts, it was suggested, on the expectation that growth would be reasonably strong in these countries. Another participant pointed out that the balance of payments of the developing countries was adversely affected not only by the impact of low economic growth in the industrial countries on the export receipts of developing countries but also by the effect of high interest rate policies in the industrial countries on the debt servicing payments of the developing countries. The balance of payments constraint could be eased in the short term by capital inflows, but this might aggravate the situation over the longer term. Nevertheless, participants remained optimistic about the growth prospects of the developing countries. They noted that the growth rate of these countries had been quite high during the late 1970s despite the slowdown in the industrial countries. They also observed that there was potential for increasing trade among the developing countries—that is, for expanding South-South trade— and suggested that this could, to some extent, replace the stimulus to growth that had been provided before the mid-1970s by trade with the industrial countries.

The Chinese Economy and Its Role in the World

Luo Yuanzheng

Recent developments in China's socialist modernization process have created a new situation. Every day, China is participating more actively in the world economy, and despite economic fluctuations throughout the world, its economy is progressing steadily. Its potential for international economic and financial cooperation is considerable. There is no doubt that China will play an increasingly greater role in the development of the world economy.

Current Economic Situation in China

Recent achievements bear witness to the steady course followed by the Chinese economy.

First, productivity is increasing at a firm pace. In 1981, the total value of industrial and agricultural output amounted to Y 749 billion, an increase of 4.5 percent, compared with 1980. The growth in agricultural production in 1981 laid the foundation for the growth of the national economy as a whole. The annual output of grain has been increasing since 1979, reaching 325 million tons in 1981. In 1981, the outputs of cotton, oil-bearing crops, sugarcane, beet, and tea were 37 percent to 96 percent higher than in 1978. During the same period, forestry, animal husbandry, fishery, and rural sideline production rose by 31 percent. In spite of natural disasters in the first half of 1982, the total output of summer grain crops is expected to exceed the 1981 level. Light industry maintained a fairly high rate of growth, with the output of cotton cloth and chemical fibers increasing by 28 percent, compared with 1978. Heavy industry picked up again after a decline, increasing by 9.5 percent in the first six months of 1982, compared with the same period of 1981. This growth rate approximated that of light industry, which was 10.7 percent. The rebound of heavy industry was due mainly to the expansion of agriculture, light industry, capital construction, and export trade, as well as to the extensive technological transformation of existing enterprises. This expansion created a need for more manufactured goods and required heavy industry to enlarge its scope of activity and adapt itself to the new situation. It proved that China's economic readjustment program in the past few years has been yielding results and that the restructuring of industry is beginning to show a favorable outcome.

Second, the financial and monetary situation is improving. For ideological and political reasons, capital construction was not curtailed rigorously several years ago. Because of this failure and because of the Government's extraordinary efforts to upgrade the standard of living in recent years, the country recorded a fiscal deficit of more than Y 10 billion in both 1979 and 1980. An economic readjustment program in 1981, however, succeeded in achieving a balance between state revenues and expenditure. During the same year, a favorable trade balance was also achieved. The total amount of bank savings in urban as well as rural areas increased markedly.

Third, the overextension in the capital construction sector is gradually being overcome. More rational and effective investments are being made. In the first half of 1982, the pace of key construction projects was quickened.

Last but not least, commodity prices have generally remained stable, domestic trade and foreign trade have increased considerably, and the standard of living continues to improve. The prices of some items have gone up in the past few years, but those of basic commodities have remained relatively unchanged. The rise in the general price index was less in 1981 than in 1980. The annual rate of growth of commodity sales in both urban and rural areas averaged 11 percent in the past three years, with the sales of luxury items, such as television sets, cassette recorders, washing machines, and refrigerators, averaging a higher rate of growth. During the same period, annual state expenditure on workers' wages, etc., increased by Y 8.2 billion. The annual net per capita income of agricultural workers rose considerably, from Y 134 in 1978 to Y 223 in 1981, an increase of 66 percent.

A New Path of Economic Development

In the 30 years following the establishment of the People's Republic of China, the State sought to develop the economy (1) by giving priority to the development of heavy industry and by gradually establishing fairly independent and comprehensive industrial and economic systems; (2) by extensively promoting economic expansion, such as the construction of new enterprises; (3) by relying mainly on domestic capital and on domestic markets while exploiting primary goods and light industry products in exchange for equipment and technology designed for heavy industry; and (4) by increasing gross social product by all means while striving to catch up with the developed capitalist countries in a short span of time.

Because of its historical inevitability, this pattern of development had outstanding merits. Flaws became apparent, however, especially in the years following the Great Leap Forward in 1958, when the blind pursuit of high productivity growth led to an inefficient pattern of production and structural imbalances. An undue stress on the development of heavy industry resulted in the neglect of agriculture and light industry, and construction and high levels of output were emphasized to the detriment of consumer goods production and the public welfare.

Since the Third Plenary Session of the Eleventh Central Committee of the Communist Party of China in 1979, China has shifted its strategy and has embarked on a path of economic development that is better adapted to its national conditions. This new path was formulated by Premier Zhao Ziyang in his report on the work of the Government delivered at the Fourth Session of the Fifth National People's Congress. He stated that it was characterized by "a fairly steady pace and better economic results, yielding more substantial benefits to the people." He also established ten guidelines by which to achieve these results.

The initial success of this policy has already created a favorable situation in the Chinese economy. The recent Twelfth National Congress of the Communist Party of China endorsed the principles and policies adopted by the Party since the Third Plenary Session of the Eleventh Central Committee. It also outlined a comprehensive plan for economic development and established priorities and short-term goals for its implementation. According to this plan, efforts will be made to quadruple the gross annual value of industrial and agricultural production from 1980 to 2000. When this goal is attained, China will be among the leading countries of the world in terms of gross national income and in terms of output of major industrial and agricultural products. It will also have considerably increased the income of its urban and rural population. Although China's national per capita income will still be relatively low, its economic strength and national defense capabilities will have grown substantially.

World Economic Situation

Since the mid-1970s, a sharp turn of events has occurred in the world economic situation. Chronic stagflation—that is, high unemployment accompanied by high inflation—has characterized the economies of the major capitalist countries. The average annual rate of growth of industrial production in the developed capitalist countries fell from 5.8 percent in the 1960s to 3.6 percent in the 1970s and, since 1979, has been deeply affected by the worldwide economic crisis. The Japanese economy, which is considered to be the strongest among the developed countries, recorded a real growth rate of only 2.7 percent in 1981. The economies of the United Kingdom and the United States have been deteriorating, and the present economic situation shows that the Western economies are still in the grip of a serious recession and that early recovery will be difficult. During the 1980s, these economies will experience the same stagflation that has haunted them since the mid-1970s.

The economic growth rate in the U.S.S.R. and the Eastern European countries has fallen since the mid-1970s; the average annual growth rate of industry in the U.S.S.R. was 5.3 percent in the 1970s, compared with 8.6 percent in the previous decade. These countries have also encountered serious economic troubles since the beginning of the 1980s. They are suffering from a shortage of financial resources and labor, and conditions for the exploitation of their resources are deteriorating. As its military expenditure increases, the economic growth rate of the U.S.S.R. is expected to drop even further.

The stagflation in the Western countries cannot but adversely affect the developing countries. As a result of the deepening economic crisis in the capitalist world since the end of the 1970s, the prices of primary goods on the world market have fallen dramatically. Trade protectionism has become common in the developed capitalist countries. These countries have reduced their aid to developing countries and forced up interest rates on the financial markets. This has created a wide range of difficulties for many developing countries.

Pressed by these difficult circumstances, the Organization of Petroleum Exporting Countries will have to come to grips with international payments deficits in 1982. In primary commodity exporting countries, which have maintained a high rate of growth for many years, the financial situation will deteriorate sharply. Their economies will slow down or decline. In many primary producing countries—especially those least developed countries whose economic structure is based on a single product—the prospects are even more discouraging. But it is our belief that, for the numerous developing countries with vast territories, a large labor supply, and abundant resources, the 1980s offer good prospects for development.

Economic Cooperation and Foreign Trade

The steady economic progress in China is in sharp contrast with the fluctuations in the rest of the world. China's drive for modernization, however, requires a favorable international environment. The global economic slump, which has created a shrinking world market, will also have an unfavorable impact on China's foreign trade. But it is China's firm intention to open its economy to the world and to increase its technological exchanges with foreign countries on the basis of equality and mutual benefit. China will continue to vigorously expand its foreign trade, make full use of all available foreign capital, and actively import advanced technologies adapted to its needs to enhance its self-reliance and to promote the development of its economy.

China's policy of opening its economy to the world, which was first adopted in 1979, has quickly helped to develop its foreign economic relations. It also offers many opportunities for economic cooperation with foreign countries. China has displayed its positive role in the world economy in five areas.

Foreign trade

China's foreign trade is expanding rapidly. The volume of world trade has stagnated since the beginning of the 1980s: it increased by

1.5 percent in 1980, only to drop by 1.6 percent the following year. There are no signs of a recovery for 1982. Trade deficits are prevalent in all Western industrial nations, except the Federal Republic of Germany and Japan. It is estimated that the oil exporting countries will reduce their volume of exports and that the non-oil developing countries will experience a further worsening of their terms of trade. In contrast to this declining world trade situation, however, China's imports and exports were 62 percent higher in 1981 than in 1979. Although the world market was sluggish and was marked by a decline in most commodity prices in the first half of 1982, China's exports amounted to US$10.2 billion, an increase of 10 percent, compared with the same period last year. Of China's export items, oil rose by 15 percent, and machinery and equipment by 19 percent.

After the United States issued its Communiqué on the Establishment of Diplomatic Relations with China in 1972, trade was quickly restored between the two countries, and China has continued to develop its commercial exchanges with the United States, especially since 1979, when diplomatic ties were formally established. Between 1972 and 1981, the total volume of their bilateral trade grew 57 times, with the total value of trade in 1981 reaching US$5.5 billion. In 1978, the U.S. share in China's foreign trade was exceeded by that of Japan and the Federal Republic of Germany, and in 1981, Japan continued to be China's major trading partner.

International financial relations

China's international financial relations are expanding, and its import of foreign capital has increased markedly. In 1980, the People's Republic of China assumed membership in the International Monetary Fund and the World Bank, and it has undertaken to fulfill its obligations to these institutions. By the end of 1981, the Bank of China had established relations with 1,071 foreign banks and their 2,920 branches in 146 countries and regions, an increase of 28 percent, compared with 1978. Because of its ample capacity for debt repayment, China enjoys high prestige in foreign capital transactions. By providing favorable terms, China has been able to raise funds since 1979. By the end of 1981, loans from foreign governments and those from international financial institutions amounted to US$5.7 billion. Of these loans, contracts valued at US$4.6 billion have been formally concluded. The Bank of China, however, has signed agreements with foreign commercial banks for a total amount of US$13 billion in available trade-related credits. The Bank, along with various Chinese departments and local enterprises, has raised US$3 billion in cash loans from foreign commercial banks.

Since 1980, the Chinese Government has approved the operation of 44 joint ventures and 425 contracts for cooperative enterprises involving both Chinese and foreign investments. The Government has also approved the supply of equipment by foreign businessmen to existing Chinese enterprises under compensatory trade, leasing, and materials processing arrangements. Japanese and French petroleum companies are cooperating with China in the exploitation of oil resources in the Bohai Sea and the Beibu Gulf in the South China Sea; these joint ventures involve US$3 billion of foreign investment. China is an ideal place for investment. There is an abundance of natural resources, the domestic market is large, wages are low, and the political situation is stable. There exist vast prospects for investment, for the import of technology, and for international economic and technological cooperation.

Energy resources

The exploration of China's abundant energy resources forms an important part of international technological and economic cooperation. Judging from present domestic supply and demand, China can rely on domestic production for its own consumption and remain independent from fluctuating prices on the world energy market. China exported 13.75 million tons of crude oil and 5.05 million tons of refined oil in 1981. China's coal is competitive on the world market, owing to its variety and high quality. The proximity of China to Japan, southeast Asia, and other regions facilitates the transport of its coal for export. Cooperation between China and Japan in the exploration and exploitation of oil in the western and southern parts of the Bohai Sea has yielded good results. China has approved the applications of 40 foreign companies to submit tenders for the joint exploitation of its offshore oil. Cooperation in the energy sector includes the joint construction of coal mines, power stations, and energy communications and transportation facilities.

As long as China's sovereignty and the principles of equality and mutual benefit are respected, we welcome this joint development of Chinese energy resources. We would also like to cooperate with other countries in the exploitation of their energy resources.

China and the developing countries

China is in favor of South-South economic cooperation and supports the efforts of the developing countries to establish a new international economic order. China can also play a major role in developing South-South cooperation. The North-South dialogue is now at a standstill. Therefore, both the trend of collective self-reliance among the developing countries and the momentum of South-South cooperation are growing. China's trade with Third World countries is expanding rapidly. It reached the equivalent of US$8.4 billion in 1980, more than five times that in 1970. In the past three years, China has cooperated with a number of Third World countries in construction projects, the supply of services, and other joint ventures. The technology provided by China is well adapted to the needs and means of Third World countries. By the same token, China can also import useful technology from other developing countries.

Economic cooperation

China's growing economy contributes to the development of the world economy. Owing to more than 30 years of effort and to a policy of self-reliance, China has established an independent and comprehensive socialist economic system. But to hasten China's modernization and to create the international economic climate conducive to this process, China is eager to establish foreign economic ties.

China in the World Economy

The serious economic depression in the developed capitalist countries and the slump in the world economy have somewhat obstructed the rapid development of China's foreign economic relations, but these developments have not been as unfavorable to China as they have been to other developing countries. China's export and import commodities are different from those of other developing countries that depend on the export of primary goods. In 1981, manufactured goods constituted 53 percent, and primary goods 37 percent, of China's exports. Therefore, the fluctuations of commodity prices on the world market, where the prices of primary goods usually fall faster than those of manufactured goods, have exerted less of an effect on China than they have on other developing countries. Along with the steady growth of the Chinese economy, China's foreign economic relations have developed steadily but rapidly. In the development of the world economy as a whole, this is a positive contribution.

In the interest of world peace and progress for mankind, China adheres to its independent foreign policy. The Chinese people cherish their friendship and cooperation with other countries and peoples. Although China will remain self-reliant, it will continue to widen its economic and technological exchanges with foreign countries to reach its long-term economic goals and, at the same time, to contribute to the development of the world economy.

Summary of Discussion

The main subjects discussed were the feasibility of the long-term growth target, the scope for easing the short-term and medium-term energy constraint on growth, and the causes of inflation in China.

One participant observed that the goal of quadrupling industrial and agricultural production by the end of this century appeared to be an ambitious one. He referred to the importance of setting realistic objectives and sought further evidence of the feasibility of the long-term growth objective and details of the way in which it would be attained. Another participant responded that experience had shown that the setting of overly ambitious growth targets could be self-defeating, as a result of the inefficiencies and imbalances caused by the attempts to reach these targets. Policymakers in China were aware of this and had thus set a goal for the next two decades that was quite attainable. The goal implied an average annual growth rate of 7.2 percent. By historical standards, this was not especially high. The comparable figure for China during 1953–81 was 8.1 percent; for the U.S.S.R. during 1956–75, it was 7.5 percent; and for Japan during 1957–70, it was 10.4 percent. In the light of these figures, China's goal appeared to be very realistic and, perhaps, even conservative.

The strategy for achieving the target involved a two-part approach. During the 1980s—and especially during 1981–85, the period covered by the five-year plan—the growth rate would be relatively low. Emphasis during this period would be placed on strengthening the economy's productive base by reducing the constraints imposed by low overall productivity and limited availability of energy. Expenditure would be shifted from investment to consumption, and productive resources would be reallocated from heavy industry to light industry. Investment would not be allowed to fall below 25 percent of national income (equivalent to about 23 percent of gross domestic product as defined by the Fund). Because the share of investment would be lower than in the late 1970s, however, increased efforts would be made to improve its efficiency and distribution. The average annual growth rate would rise as the needed readjustments were made and would exceed 7.2 percent during the 1990s. It was pointed out that the greater importance attached to consumption, as well as the adoption of measures to strengthen work incentives, had won popular support for the Government's growth program, and it was suggested that this support provided the strongest guarantee that the objectives of the program would be attained.

Several references were made to the importance of energy supplies for maintaining rapid economic growth and to possible ways in which these supplies might be increased. Among the latter was a suggestion that China reduce its net exports of oil. Another participant argued that, while there might be some scope for doing this, it was limited by the existence of long-term contracts with several countries. He pointed out that other approaches to easing the energy constraint would also be followed, including exploitation of opportunities for conservation in the short run and increased production of coal, hydroelectricity, and offshore oil in the medium term and long term.

It was observed that inflationary pressures need not always manifest themselves immediately in rising prices but could take the form of shortages of factors of production and of goods and services. Some participants argued that bottlenecks and rationing indicated that China was experiencing some inflation, though it was probably much less severe than in other developing countries and in many industrial countries. The causes of this inflation could be attributed to uneven economic policies adopted during the Cultural Revolution and also, perhaps, to excessive increases in the money supply.

Fund Programs
for Economic Adjustment

Manuel Guitián

The International Monetary Fund seeks to promote economic cooperation among its member countries as a means of fostering the growth of international trade so that high levels of employment and real income can be attained in the world economy. An essential aspect of the role and activities of the institution is the provision of financial assistance to countries that face actual or potential balance of payments difficulties. Access to the resources of the Fund is granted to support the efforts of member countries to solve their balance of payments problems by the pursuit of policies that take into account both their own interests and those of the membership as a whole. This paper describes, in broad terms, the logical framework of the policies and practices developed in the Fund over a period of more than three decades to govern the use of its resources by member countries undertaking an adjustment effort.

The policies and procedures of the Fund in this particular area are similar to those the Fund has developed in its other fields of competence, such as surveillance over exchange rates and exchange practices or consultations procedures, and they are applicable to all members. More specifically, the implementation of Fund policies is independent of the particular system or line of economic and institutional organization that characterizes individual member countries. This independence, however, should not be interpreted as implying either disregard for or neglect of a member's special characteristics and institutional setting. On the contrary, in its relations with members, the Fund has always been particularly mindful of the individual features and institutions of a member's economy.

The importance that the Fund attaches to issues that derive from the special traits of each member country was made explicit and formalized in a recent decision of the Executive Board on the access of members to the general resources of the Fund. Periodically, the Board undertakes broad reviews of what has come to be known in international financial circles as the "conditionality practices of the Fund," that is, the conditions that the Fund attaches to the use of its resources. Such conditions are directly related to the economic policies that the Fund expects members to follow when they request financial assistance from the institution. The last general review of this subject was conducted during 1978–79 and concluded on March 2, 1979 with the adoption by the Executive Board of a decision containing guidelines on conditionality. This decision, in its fourth paragraph, includes the following statement:

> . . . In helping members to devise adjustment programs, the Fund will pay due regard to the domestic social and political objectives, the economic priorities, and the circumstances of members, including the causes of their balance of payments problems.[1]

Compliance with this guideline calls for flexibility on the part of the Fund in its efforts to promote adjustment by those members facing actual or potential balance of payments difficulties. It is through the careful exercise of flexibility that the individual aspects of a member's economy and its institutional setting can be taken into consideration.

The guideline quoted above represents no more than an extension to the area of economic adjustment of a general principle that is spelled out in the Articles of Agreement—the institution's basic charter—in connection with the Fund's role in the broader field of surveillance over foreign exchange arrangements, which is a critical responsibility of the institution. The Articles of Agreement prescribe that the principles adopted by the Fund for purposes of surveillance

> shall respect the domestic social and political policies of members, and in applying these principles the Fund shall pay due regard to the circumstances of members.[2]

Both quotations make a common reference to the need to pay due

---

[1] Executive Board Decision No. 6056-(79/38), adopted March 2, 1979, *Selected Decisions of the International Monetary Fund and Selected Documents*, Ninth Issue (Washington, June 15, 1981), p. 20.

[2] Article IV, Section 3(b).

regard, inter alia, to "the circumstances of members." In the words of Joseph Gold, former General Counsel and Director of the Legal Department of the Fund, "'the circumstances of members' is a phrase of panoramic scope."[3] Such a scope encompasses the acceptance by the Fund of a member's economic organization as given, as an issue beyond debate.

The scope for the exercise of flexibility by the Fund in its relations and operations with members, however, is not limitless. To begin with, there is the general set of obligations that countries undertake to observe when they become members of the Fund: their acceptance to uphold the objectives and goals of the institution, which confines each member's freedom of action within the bounds that are imposed by the interests of the membership as a whole. In addition, there is a more specific constraint that the Fund—in common with most other collective bodies—is required to observe: the principle of uniformity of treatment to ensure that the institution's relationships with members are—and are perceived to be—evenhanded. Simultaneous observance of the principles of flexibility and uniformity of treatment requires the achievement of a delicate balance between the two. From the standpoint of the Fund, uniform treatment cannot be properly attained by disregarding the particular features and specific situations of members. On the other hand, an unconstrained exercise of flexibility, besides being arbitrary, cannot but render the principle of uniform treatment meaningless.

Concept and Characteristics of an Imbalance

For the general purpose of this paper, it is only necessary to outline a concept of economic imbalance from the most abstract perspective possible, thereby avoiding the complications that arise in the actual implementation of policy. To this end, the issue of adjustment is addressed here by focusing on the notion of an actual or potential adjustment need. A convenient dimension of this starting point is that, by definition, it does not depend on the specific features of an economy.

---

[3] See Joseph Gold, *Conditionality*, IMF Pamphlet Series, No. 31 (Washington, 1979), p. 23.

Conceptually, a need for adjustment can be said to exist whenever total claims or demands on resources exceed the aggregate amount of resources that is available domestically and from abroad. Global imbalances of the sort that correspond to this broad definition arise periodically in most economies. In the effort to cope with them, policymakers often attempt to ascertain the specific causes of these imbalances. Frequently, the attempts are aimed at establishing whether the causes of the imbalances are external or internal in origin, or whether they are exogenous or endogenous in nature. From the viewpoint of the formulation of economic policy decisions, it may be useful to determine whether the origin of a disequilibrium lies in developments within the country's economy or in events that took place elsewhere in the world. Similarly, the strategy adopted to avert or correct an imbalance may be influenced by whether the imbalance has been created by domestic policies—that is, by whether it is endogenous—or by whether it is independent of those policies—that is, by whether it is exogenous.

Investigation of these aspects of the source of an imbalance is useful. For the design of an adjustment effort, however, the critical issue revolves around a different aspect of the imbalance: the determination of whether its causes are transitory or permanent. The answer given to this question largely determines whether or not adjustment is required. Imbalances or deficits that are due to transient factors can be expected to be self-correcting, and perhaps also reversible. From this perspective, the origin and the nature of the imbalances are of secondary importance. Temporary imbalances, ceteris paribus, need not call for any, or at most call for relatively minor, policy modifications. If, in addition, they are reversible, such imbalances require only temporary financing; borrowing abroad or use of international reserves or a combination of both would be appropriate responses to them.

When the imbalances are caused by permanent factors, however, there is no alternative to adjustment. Continued reliance on financing will not eliminate the disequilibrium; at best, it can only serve to postpone adjustment. In this context, it is worth stressing that resort to restrictions on the freedom to engage in economic transactions, including transactions involving foreign exchange, only serves to suppress the imbalance. This course of action usually gives economic agents incentives to seek ways to circumvent the restrictions, thereby giving rise to problems of efficiency and, probably, of equity as well. It is true that an imbalance can sometimes be temporarily repressed in an economy by the use of restrictions and controls. Basically, such a strategy amounts to an attempt to close the economy from the rest of the world, thereby forfeiting the potential benefits that arise from international transactions. But additionally, during the period when the controls are effective, the pressures that then cannot be released elsewhere turn inward and aggravate the original imbalance. As a result, further increases in the restrictiveness of the system are likely to be required. Clearly, such a setting cannot but be inimical to economic efficiency.

By assisting members in need of adjustment, the Fund seeks to remove the imbalances, that is, to restore a sustainable relationship between the aggregate demand for and the supply of resources. Uniformity of treatment requires that, for a given degree of need, the adjustment effort sought by the Fund be broadly equivalent among members. Flexibility of treatment is ensured by tailoring the objectives and instruments of the adjustment program to the circumstances, priorities, and characteristics of the country.

As with the search for both uniformity and flexibility, the Fund in its programs to redress economic imbalances aims at achieving a reasonable balance between adjustment and financing, both of which can and should be mutually supporting. Adjustment and financing can be described as the two sides of the seesaw that a Fund program always contains. This reflects the awareness that, in the presence of an imbalance, adjustment without financing is disruptive and costly, on the one hand, and that financing without adjustment is untenable, on the other. In seeking to define a sustainable path of adjustment, Fund programs actually look for the optimal amount of financing. In one sense, an important aspect of the concept of sustainability is its very close relationship with the availability of financing. This particular relationship has been given operational meaning in the linkage made in Fund arrangements between performance under the program (the adjustment aspect) and drawings on the resources of the Fund (the financing aspect).

Avoidance and Resolution of Imbalances

The economic programs supported by the Fund with its resources always contain measures to avert or to correct an external imbalance.

As argued earlier, this objective entails the maintenance or restoration of a sustainable relationship between the demand for resources and the supply that is actually available to the economy. Therefore, whatever strategy is chosen, the program must contain measures that act either on the demand for resources, the supply of resources, or both.

At the risk of oversimplification, the various economic policy measures required to effect an adjustment can be classified according to where they appear to have their most direct and strongest impact. Some measures typically influence the level and the composition of aggregate demand. Others aim at affecting the rate and the structure of production, that is, the level and composition of aggregate supply. In reality, a caveat is required, however; groupings such as those just outlined are not clear cut because all economic variables tend to be interdependent and, therefore, do not lend themselves to unambiguous classification.

Policies and measures of domestic demand management can be distinguished according to their fiscal and monetary nature. Again at the risk of oversimplification, this particular distinction can be explained as follows. There is a very close relationship between the level and the rate of growth of demand and those of expenditure in any economy. Consequently, one method of managing domestic demand can be through adequate monitoring of expenditure that, in many instances, calls for strict control of one major component of total expenditure: government or public sector spending. Fund experience with a large variety of members over a long period indicates that this source of expenditure is often behind unsustainable expansions in aggregate demand.

Excessive total expenditure in an economy can be brought under control directly by curtailing public sector spending—one of its main components—or indirectly by raising additional fiscal revenues. The indirect revenue route will not reduce public sector spending, but it will tend to dampen private expenditure so that the overall level or rate of growth of demand is lowered. These policy options can be grouped under the general label of the "fiscal aspect" of demand management. In brief, this particular aspect of demand management seeks to limit the size of a fiscal or public sector deficit to the amount of noninflationary financing available in the economy.

A second method of controlling aggregate demand is based on the relationship that exists between total spending and domestic borrowing. Excess expenditure in an economy in general, and in the public sector in particular, can of course be sustained whenever borrowing can be undertaken. In itself, there is nothing wrong with borrowing; actually, borrowing is the process that allows the transfer of resources among economic agents over space and time. However, as in all other economic areas, balance must also be observed in the process of borrowing. The very presence of an excessive level of expenditure financed by borrowing implies—as it were, by definition—that the demand for borrowed resources surpasses the supply of available resources. In the domestic economic sphere, these relationships between expenditure levels and domestic borrowing possibilities are what can be termed "the monetary aspect" of demand management. Briefly, this aspect simply postulates that the level of domestic spending can be checked by the establishment of domestic credit policies that ensure broad balance between the demand for and the supply of domestic financial resources in general, and for credit and money in particular.

There are also policies and measures that belong in the area of supply management. In general, it can be argued that aggregate supply issues allow for less direct treatment and resolution than those relating to aggregate demand. This is because supply responses to policy action are unlikely to be as rapid as those that can be elicited from the demand side. Realization of supply potential requires efficiency in resource allocation, which, in turn, depends on the prevalence of appropriate economic incentives. Supply is also contingent on the amount of available resources, and in this context, the whole area of external debt management is of particular importance. While foreign borrowing can serve to circumvent demand management and domestic credit policies (e.g., by financing excessive expenditure on domestic goods and services without necessarily adding to their supply), it can also be instrumental in increasing the supply of resources available to an economy (e.g., by allowing for more imports of goods and services). The critical point in the supply context is the scope that the availability of foreign savings (i.e., foreign borrowing) can provide to domestic economic management by supplementing domestic savings and thereby allowing for the attainment of investment levels and real growth rates that otherwise would be unattainable. This line of reasoning makes clear how important it is to ensure that borrowing from abroad be undertaken in amounts and on terms that are sustainable. Or, to put it differently, it also makes clear how critical it is to ensure that the foreign savings be invested productively so that the economy can service its external debt in an orderly manner, that is, without experiencing foreign debt servicing difficulties.

In the supply context, the broad area of economic incentives and prices, including the exchange rate and interest rates, can hardly be overemphasized. Attention needs to be drawn to the role that prices in general play in any economy in conveying information on the relative scarcity of resources and the degree of preference for existing commodities. The issue at stake here is not the particular method of formation of prices but their critical importance for any system of economic organization. A relative price structure based on the scarcity value of resources and also representative of the structure of demand can maximize the efficiency of resource allocation and thereby the level of output that is to be distributed in the economy.

In this area, emphasis can be placed on the following variables: the exchange rate, which is of direct interest to the Fund not only from a general economic perspective but also from a jurisdictional standpoint; interest rates, which can be crucial for the attainment of balance of payments, development, and growth objectives; and the prices of goods and services of particular importance to the economy, because these also can have significant impacts in the financial, allocational, and distributional spheres.

In a very summary fashion, an overvalued currency not only constrains domestic output unduly by placing export production at a disadvantage, but it also typically influences aggregate demand in the wrong direction by subsidizing imports. In these circumstances, the economy is forced to resort more and more to either foreign borrowing (usually on increasingly hard terms), or use of its foreign reserves (which are, of course, exhaustible), or both. These events are often accompanied simultaneously or eventually, as the case may be, by the introduction or intensification of exchange and trade restrictions, that is, by effectively closing the economy. Experience shows, however, that restrictions lead to the proliferation of unofficial markets, which make it difficult to close the economy completely. Thus, restrictions cannot remove indefinitely the need to correct the imbalance by means of appropriate adjustment measures.

As with the exchange rate, an inadequate domestic interest rate contributes to balance of payments pressures by encouraging both capital outflows and domestic spending. But even more important, over the longer term, such interest rates discourage savings and impair the efficiency of investments. Thus, they tend to reduce the economy's potential for development and growth and, consequently, to weaken the balance of payments. Also, setting economically low prices for key commodities and services typically reduces efficiency and leads to financial imbalances. Frequently, the subsidies that the pricing policies seek to create do not benefit the sectors for which they are intended. All these arguments stress the importance of promoting efficiency in any economic setting, an objective that generally calls for strengthening, rather than weakening, price incentives.

Evolution of Fund Practices

The general practices that have evolved to guide the use of Fund resources have come to encompass all the aspects of economic policies that affect the demand and supply sides of an economy. The broad aim of these practices is the attainment and maintenance of a reasonable balance between these two sides in the context of a liberal system of multilateral payments to enable members to derive the benefits that flow from the voluntary interaction of their economies on the basis of a mutually agreed code of conduct. This general and all-encompassing objective is viewed as the most likely to provide for price level and balance of payments stability together with high and sustainable rates of economic development and growth.

In the search for the appropriate blend between adjustment and financing, the Fund has established a variety of instruments and facilities to make its resources available to members with actual or potential balance of payments needs. The use of those resources has been made subject to different degrees of conditionality; these differences are intended to reflect the different characteristics of the balance of payments problems of members. In general, it must be pointed out that, to a larger or a lesser degree, all uses of Fund resources are conditional; from this perspective, the provision of Fund financial assistance, in all its manifestations, is always aimed at supporting members' adjustment efforts. But the existence of varying degrees of conditionality allows for a classification of existing Fund facilities under two major headings: on the one side, facilities with a bias toward financing; and on the other, facilities with a bias toward adjustment.

The facilities with a bias toward financing either do not require members to undertake a specific policy program or require only a broad description of such a program for members to have access to the resources of the facility. Those that do not necessarily require an explicit policy program include the compensatory financing facility, the buffer stock financing facility, and the temporary 1974 oil facility. A general description of a policy program is required to make members eligible to draw ordinary resources from the Fund in an amount equivalent to the first credit tranche (i.e., drawings that would raise the Fund's holdings of a member's currency from 100 percent to 125 percent of its quota). Such a description of a program of policy action was also required of members requesting loans from the already lapsed 1975 oil facility and the Trust Fund.

Access to resources in the higher credit tranches and to resources from the extended Fund facility, the supplementary financing facility, and its successor, the enlarged access policy, are biased in favor of adjustment. Such a bias is illustrated, on the one hand, by the requirement that the measures and policies included in programs supported by these types of Fund resources be quantified—in what are called performance criteria—to allow for a measurement of perform- ance and, on the other, by the phasing of financial assistance in installments that are made available only when the agreed criteria have been observed. In reality, the implementation of these practices is more flexible than is generally thought. The performance criteria, in effect, play the role of precautionary signals that ensure that the situation is reviewed whenever the performance of the economy is not on track. While in the interim the member is not entitled to make drawings from the Fund, the technique of linking performance to disbursements allows for a determination of whether the deviation that occurred was unimportant—in which case a waiver is granted for the lack of observance of the performance criterion and the member can proceed to draw on the Fund—or whether adaptations of policies are required—in which case the performance criteria are modified by mutual agreement and the member's drawing rights are thereby restored.

This classification of financial assistance under the various Fund facilities overemphasizes the contrast that actually exists among them.

While it is indeed accurate to say that the degree of conditionality is higher under one group of facilities than under the other, attention must also be drawn to the differences that exist in the magnitude of the assistance that each group of facilities can make available. Leaving aside the facilities that have lapsed (e.g., the oil facilities), at present, the combined drawings under the compensatory and the buffer stock financing facilities cannot exceed the equivalent of 175 percent of quota. In contrast, potential drawings under the more conditional facilities (i.e., under credit tranche policies and the extended Fund facility) can amount to an average of 150 percent of quota a year over a period of three years, for a total of 450 percent of quota, subject to an absolute maximum of 600 percent of quota. Therefore, while the policy conditions may be stricter in stand-by and extended arrangements, the financial support that those arrangements can offer to members that have entered into them is substantially larger than the assistance that can be provided to members that have resort only to the less conditional facilities. From this perspective, perhaps the best classification of the facilities is somewhat paradoxical: on the one hand, there are facilities with a bias toward financing but which can only provide relatively limited financial assistance; and, on the other hand, there are facilities with a bias toward adjustment but which offer assistance from the Fund on a substantial scale.

Some Issues in the Context of Adjustment

Two different kinds of issues can arise in the context of adjustment programs supported by the Fund. First, there are issues of a general nature that address important aspects of the adjustment process. Second, there are issues related to the complexities that arise in the context of the Fund's approach to adjustment as a result of the diverse institutional settings and characteristics of its members.

Two general issues are particularly controversial: the appropriate speed of adjustment and the proper measurement of the efficiency of adjustment. The speed of adjustment is an issue that has not yet been, and perhaps cannot be, conclusively resolved. It is frequently described as a choice between a "shock" approach and a "gradual" approach to the adjustment process. This choice, however, is not unconstrained. Its limits are determined by the relationship mentioned earlier between adjustment and financing. There is a constraint on the choice of approach that is imposed by the linkage between the size of the imbalance, on the one hand, and the availability of finance, on the other. This relationship serves to gauge the adjustment need as well as the extent of the adjustment effort. The issue has not yet been resolved because, even in those instances where financing is available, it is not always obvious that a gradual process of adjustment is preferable to a rapid one. [4]

The issue of the measurement of the efficiency of the adjustment effort or, in other words, the assessment of economic performance, is also a complex one. In the normal process of learning by doing, it is important to be in a position to ascertain which are the proper methods and standards for evaluating economic performance. Here only three possible standards of measurement are discussed. The first could be called a positive or factual standard in that it relates the results of policies to the situation that prevailed in the economy prior to their introduction: that is, it measures *what is* relative to *what was*. The second is a normative standard that compares actual policy results with policy targets: this entails a comparison of *what is* with *what ought to be*. The third is a conjectural standard that compares actual policy results vis-à-vis the events that would have occurred in the absence of—or in the presence of a different set of—policies: this standard compares *what is* with *what would or could have been*. All three standards can be useful, but their usefulness is not independent of the judgments—in particular, the value judgments—of the observer.

Issues also arise as a result of the diversity of the Fund's membership, including differences in systems of economic organization. Many of the Fund's policies and practices have been derived from an analytical framework in which an important degree of decentralized economic decision making was the norm rather than the exception. But this does not mean that the basic rationale of those policies and practices does not apply in environments where decision making is more centralized. To begin with, the basic problem addressed by Fund policies is common to all members' economics, regardless of their particular economic setting; specifically, external imbalances and the

---

[4] The choice between shock and gradual strategies of adjustment is only meaningful with respect to economic policies. As far as the results of the policies themselves are concerned, gradualism is inevitable regardless of the particular choice that is made because even a shock-type approach will typically take time to yield results.

inevitability of adjustment are independent of the degree of centralization of decision making that prevails in an economy. Also, the benefits to be derived from efficiency in resource allocation and from the existence of economic interaction among member countries are independent of the pattern of economic organization. Last but not least, the Fund objective of ensuring that the adjustment process leads to an environment where both stability and development can be attained is valid for all types of economies.

The concept of "balance of payments need" is important for understanding the circumstances under which a member may have access to Fund assistance. Any actual use of Fund resources requires the member to demonstrate that it has a balance of payments need for those resources. Formally, such a requirement entails an obligation of the member to represent that it has a need to draw on the resources of the Fund "because of its balance of payments or its reserve position or developments in its reserves" (Article V, Section 3(b)(ii)). From an operational standpoint, "balance of payments need" is more of a term of art than a precisely measurable concept. As its formal description makes clear, the establishment of the existence of such a need involves judgments that encompass factors such as the size of and developments in a country's international reserves as well as its balance of payments position. Balance of payments needs (which in the context of a member's request for the use of conditional Fund resources can be either actual or prospective) emerge or are expected to emerge as a result of external or internal developments, including inappropriate domestic policies. Indeed, one of the purposes of the financial assistance provided by the Fund is to eliminate or avert the balance of payments need by removing its causes or by helping the economy to adjust to them.

In a centrally planned economy, the balance of payments need may be implicit in the decisions made on expenditure in general, or on investment in particular. From this standpoint, it can be argued that the balance of payments need is a planned outcome, an objective being deliberately sought, rather than a result of actions that require modification or correction. For purposes of Fund financing, the notion of balance of payments need corresponds more to the idea of a consequence of, say, certain past or prospective policy actions than to the idea of an objective embodied in those actions. It is for this reason that an adjustment effort supported by the Fund typically calls for new policy measures or for modifications to existing policies in order to eliminate the causes of the external imbalance. In other words, a country that is ready to engage in an adjustment effort and, on this basis, requests assistance from the Fund in fact undertakes to eliminate or to avert its balance of payments need over a foreseeable period of time. Thus, in the context of a centrally planned economy, a conflict may arise whenever the policy strategy in the global plan involves both a planned balance of payments deficit and Fund assistance to support an adjustment effort, because this effort would in most circumstances entail a modification of certain policies included in the plan.

A second area of interest is the appropriate framing of the adjustment program where an actual or potential balance of payments need has arisen. In economies where decision making is centralized, there is probably more scope for the use of direct measures of adjustment than in economies where decisions are decentralized. Thus, although the requirements of an adjustment effort can be the same for both types of economies, the instruments of adjustment may differ. [5]

Some of the performance criteria typically included in Fund programs, such as those covering external debt management and exchange and trade restrictions, apply to all economies, regardless of their lines of organization. But certain others, such as limits on the total amount of domestic credit or on the expansion of bank credit to the public sector, may be less useful for a centralized economy, where limits on global public sector expenditure might provide a more direct route to demand management.

In general, in a centrally planned economy there are normally direct means to control aggregate demand and, at least in principle, such control can be exercised more effectively than in a decentralized economy. The offset to this particular advantage of a centralized system appears to be in the supply of goods and services. In such a system, economic decisions—and particularly, pricing decisions—are administrative, and the attainment of supply potential is by no means assured. Achievement of supply potential revolves around the whole area of relative prices, exchange rates, and interest rates that were discussed earlier. The relevance of pricing in the process of economic

---

[5] In this context, it is worth emphasizing the critical importance of timely statistical information to understand the workings of the economy and to be able to follow and assess its performance.

calculation for purposes of achieving efficiency in production and of providing information on the structure of demand in all types of economies has been recognized and subject to extensive treatment in the economic literature.[6]

In general, it is useful to view an arrangement with the Fund as an instrument for facilitating and reinforcing the process of domestic economic policymaking. From this standpoint, it is in the interest of both the member and the Fund that adjustment programs be formulated in terms of the most appropriate instruments and that there be a sufficient flow of information not only to design the program but also to follow its implementation and assess its results.

Concluding Remarks

In concluding this paper, I would like to emphasize the importance of safeguarding the universal character of the Fund. This particular dimension requires that all countries that are able and willing to abide by the prescriptions of the Articles of Agreement can join its ranks, regardless of any differences that may exist in their economic features or systems of economic organization. This universality of accession has been strengthened by the Fund's practice of avoiding distinctions among groups of member countries, a practice that is in line with the Articles of Agreement, which prescribe rights and obligations that apply equally to all members.

As pointed out earlier, this should not be interpreted as meaning that the Fund is impervious to country differences. The diversity that exists among member countries in terms of the stage of their economic development, the degree of openness of their economies, or the extent of centralization in economic decision making is generally recognized, particularly in those areas where such diversity either has or can have important implications for policies of balance of payments adjustment. The need to strike a balance between uniformity and flexibility calls for a careful exercise of judgment. While it is true that uniformity, properly conceived, requires a degree of flexibility, such a conception

---

[6] In the context of a centrally planned economy, see, for example, Mark Allen, "Adjustment in Planned Economies," *Staff Papers*, International Monetary Fund (Washington), Vol. 29 (September 1982), pp. 398–421, and the references listed there.

does not go as far as to allow for unfettered flexibility because this would run counter to the proper functioning of a cooperative entity like the Fund.

In the area of adjustment and use of Fund resources, there is ample scope for such an exercise of judgment. Priorities differ between centralized and decentralized economies. Indeed, the differences go a long way toward explaining the reasons for the existence of the two types of economic system. But it must also be acknowledged that there are important areas of similarity, such as, as has already been noted, the existence from time to time of imbalances and the need to adjust those of a persistent nature. These are common realities to all economies. On a different but related plane, the achievement of economic efficiency is also a common objective among members. Different priorities may lead to different solutions to the problem of inefficiency, but the differences that may exist do not extend to the acceptance of resource waste.

As far as adjustment policies in Fund programs are concerned, this paper has addressed only very sketchily a few of the issues that arise in the context of economies differentiated on the basis of the degree of centralization. Some of the complexities that surround a basic concept such as a balance of payments need have been indicated. Even more difficult issues arise with respect to restrictions and exchange rates. All of these encompass obviously difficult questions. But they should not deflect attention from the basic objective to which adjustment efforts and Fund financial assistance are aimed: the attainment of a viable balance of payments position in a context of price and exchange rate stability so as to foster the process of development and growth.

If there is general agreement with the desirability of this objective, then it follows that all members have an interest in averting emerging imbalances or correcting those that already prevail in the most efficient fashion. This interest is common to the member experiencing the imbalance and to the rest of the membership if only because of the increasingly close interdependence that links the economies of members. The presence of an institution like the Fund attests to this interdependence and to the existence of interests that are common to the whole membership. But general interest in the adjustment of imbalances does not mean that such an adjustment has to be effected in a single and predetermined fashion. The only constraints that bind the strategies for adjustment are those specified in the Articles of

Agreement, to which all members are signatories and which all members have, therefore, undertaken to observe.

In the particular context of the centralized economies, and subject to institutional constraints or to those constraints imposed by the code of conduct laid out in the Articles of Agreement, this means that the design of an adjustment effort should be based on those instruments that appear most appropriate in the context of their organizational setting. It is typical in these economies that the share of the government in the system as a whole is larger than is the case in less centralized economies. As a result, it is likely that the degree of government influence over the main macroeconomic variables (such as demand, expenditure, consumption, and investment) is substantial so that whenever these economies move onto an unsustainable path, equilibrium can be restored in a relatively rapid and direct manner. To the extent that this is the case, performance criteria dealing directly with these variables could conceivably be used in lieu of the more conventional but indirect instruments such as credit ceilings typically used in arrangements between the Fund and members with market-oriented economies.

In principle, to the extent that detailed planning techniques are used and detailed objectives are sought in centralized economies, adjustment would be best framed in the context of the overall plan; that is, the adjustment effort should be an integral part of the plan. This is not to say that, in the process of negotiating an arrangement, the Fund would need to enter into all aspects of the plan. Once again, judgment is called for, but it can be surmised that the Fund's interest would normally be limited to those areas that have a bearing on its jurisdictional responsibilities (e.g., exchange practices) or on the major objectives of the adjustment (e.g., the balance of payments). The goal of keeping Fund involvement in the process of policy formulation broadly uniform and comparable among members is complex, but it can be attained. In fact, this is explicitly recognized in the guidelines on conditionality, in particular, in the guideline quoted at the outset of this paper which calls for due regard to be paid to the social and political priorities of members. This thought is also behind the prescription included in another of the guidelines that states that the number and content of performance criteria may vary depending on the diversity of problems and institutional arrangements of members, subject to the requirement that the number of performance criteria must be limited to those necessary to evaluate the implementation of the program. In general, it can be said that the rules that the Fund follows in applying its conditionality practices are broad enough to encompass all types of economies.

This paper has also pointed out the critical importance that must be attached to the provision of information on a timely basis. This is not only essential to improve the understanding of how a centralized economy actually operates but it is also the only reasonable grounds on which to formulate adjustment objectives. Information is also likely to be crucial in the area of supply potential and resource allocation. The supply side is of particular importance to centrally planned economies to ensure that the objectives on production that have been built into the plan do not depart excessively from the long-run interests of the community. In other words, the structure of production that has been built into the plan cannot be made completely separate from the structure of demand, even if aggregate demand is subject to an important degree of control. The role that information plays in this area can hardly be overstressed. This information is conveyed in some economies via market prices; in other economies, via shadow prices, queues, and unsalable inventories. But, in the final analysis, the particular channel through which information is made available is immaterial. What counts is that the information be accurate and put to good use.

Related Reading

Allen, Mark, "Adjustment in Planned Economies," *Staff Papers*, International Monetary Fund (Washington), Vol. 29 (September 1982), pp. 398–421.

Brau, Eduard, "The Consultation Process of the Fund," *Finance & Development*, International Monetary Fund and World Bank (Washington), Vol. 18 (December 1981), pp. 13–16.

Finch, C. David, "Adjustment Policies and Conditionality," in *IMF Conditionality*, ed. by John Williamson (Washington), scheduled to be published in 1983.

Gold, Joseph, *The Stand-By Arrangements of the International Monetary Fund: A Commentary on their Formal, Legal, and Financial Aspects* (Washington, 1970).

—————, *Conditionality*, IMF Pamphlet Series, No. 31 (Washington, 1979).

Guitián, Manuel, "Fund Conditionality and the International Adjustment Process: The Early Period, 1950–70," *Finance & Development*, International Monetary Fund and World Bank (Washington), Vol. 17 (December 1980), pp. 23–27.

———, "Fund Conditionality and the International Adjustment Process: The Changing Environment of the 1970s," *Finance & Development*, International Monetary Fund and World Bank (Washington), Vol. 18 (March 1981), pp. 8–11.

———, "Fund Conditionality and the International Adjustment Process: A Look into the 1980s," *Finance & Development*, International Monetary Fund and World Bank (Washington), Vol. 18 (June 1981), pp. 14–17.

———, *Fund Conditionality: Evolution of Principles and Practices*, IMF Pamphlet Series, No. 38 (Washington, 1981).

———, "Economic Management and International Monetary Fund Conditionality," in *Adjustment and Financing in the Developing World: The Role of the International Monetary Fund*, ed. by Tony Killick (Washington, 1982), pp. 73–104.

International Monetary Fund, *The Monetary Approach to the Balance of Payments: A Collection of Research Papers by Members of the Staff of the International Monetary Fund* (Washington, 1977).

———, *Articles of Agreement* (Washington, 1978).

———, *Selected Decisions of the International Monetary Fund and Selected Documents*, Ninth Issue (Washington, June 15, 1981).

Mookerjee, Subimal, "New Guidelines for Use of Fund Resources Follow Review of Practice of Conditionality," *IMF Survey* (Washington), Vol. 8 (March 19, 1979), pp. 82–83.

Robichek, E. Walter, "Financial Programming: Stand-By Arrangements and Stabilization Programs" (unpublished, International Monetary Fund, January 6, 1971).

Summary of Discussion

Participants regarded the adjustment programs supported by the Fund with its resources as being generally helpful to countries seeking to strengthen their balance of payments. Some suggested that this assistance probably played a more important role in market-oriented economies, since these economies were more likely to experience external imbalances than were centrally planned economies. It was also argued that the activities of the international commercial banks could be inimical to smooth adjustment, that the Fund's conditionality practices should take into account the origin of a member's payments difficulties, and that the Fund might sometimes be exceeding its terms of reference when it asked countries to undertake difficult adjustment programs.

The ways in which the Fund's 146 members organized their economies covered a wide spectrum, from market economies where decisions with respect to the level, composition, and mode of production were mostly decentralized to a number of nonmarket economies where most of those decisions were highly centralized. Participants noted that, while the view that payments imbalances could not arise in nonmarket economies was clearly refuted by experience, it was nevertheless true that such imbalances were less likely to occur in nonmarket than in market economies, if only because decisions about production in the former were subject to central control.

The Fund staff argued that external imbalances were independent of the method used for making decisions about production. An imbalance arose whenever there was an excess of aggregate demand over aggregate supply, and this could occur in both market and nonmarket economies. There might, however, be differences in the speed with which imbalances became apparent and in the form in which imbalances appeared in the two types of economy. In the market economies, any global disequilibrium quickly manifested itself in the form of accelerating prices and imports. In the nonmarket economies, an imbalance might not become obvious for some time, but it eventually would become apparent as shortages increased and restrictions intensified.

Disturbances that gave rise to external imbalances could be distinguished according to whether they were within or outside the control of the authorities. Some participants observed that the large rise in the current account deficit of the non-oil developing countries since the early 1970s could be attributed to two factors: the increases in the oil import bill and the rising interest payments on the external debts of these countries. They argued that, as both factors causing the deficits were of external origin, it was unfair to expect the non-oil developing countries to adopt strong adjustment programs to correct them.

The Fund staff suggested that the important distinction for determining whether or not a payments imbalance gave rise to a need for policy action depended on whether its causes were temporary or permanent. A temporary cause, such as a drought that reduced output of a major export crop below its trend level, required financing rather than adjustment.* In contrast, a permanent cause, regardless of its origin, called for adjustment. If a country suffered a permanent decline in its terms of trade, which gave rise to an unsustainable current account deficit, the country would have to undertake an adjustment effort. This applied whether the deterioration in the terms of trade was due to ill-conceived domestic policies or, for example, to technological changes abroad. If the country did not respond to the disturbance by making appropriate policy changes, adjustment would be imposed on it when its international reserves were exhausted and its borrowing power had disappeared. In this case, the compression of imports would be sudden and substantial and could be expected to produce considerable economic dislocation and welfare loss. Alternatively, the authorities could design the path along which adjustment would take place, and thus implement an adjustment program to protect the economy from abrupt and unnecessary hardships.

Concern was expressed about one side effect that was perceived when a stand-by or an extended arrangement between the Fund and a member country ran into difficulties and when the latter's right to request further drawings was interrupted. It was noted that, when this occurred, the commercial banks also tended to reduce their lending to that country, thereby imposing an additional burden on the country at the very time that its need for additional support had increased.

The Fund staff suggested that foreign commercial banks and other sources of international capital tended to restrain their lending when doubts arose about a country's creditworthiness, which at times might be related to the existence of an arrangement that was not on track. These institutions would be less likely to reduce their lending if there were a better understanding of the meaning of a country's temporary interruption of the right to draw under an arrangement with the Fund. They pointed out that, when a member sought an arrangement with the Fund, it accompanied its request with a letter of intent that included a quantitative description of the adjustment path that the member's authorities expected the economy to follow. Drawings were related to the movement of the economy along the indicated path. When the economy deviated from that path, the most appropriate course of action was to review the situation to determine whether or not any policy changes were needed. If they were, then the Fund could discuss with the member the form these changes should take so that when agreement on the policy modifications was reached the member's right to request drawings would be restored. Should policy changes not be required—and this was frequently the case—the Fund normally granted a waiver to restore the member's drawing rights immediately. Were financial institutions to appreciate more fully that loss by a country of its right to draw was not, in itself, necessarily a cause for particular concern, they would be less inclined to reduce their lending to the country.

It was also noted that, while the commercial banks might react to the interruption of Fund lending to a country by reducing their own lending, the reverse relationship did not hold, that is, the Fund did not stop supporting a country when the commercial banks stopped lending to it. In many cases, it was often at this stage that the Fund commenced lending, because it was only then that many countries turned to the Fund for assistance.

In this context, it was also pointed out that an arrangement with the Fund frequently increased the flow of commercial bank lending to a country, or at least prevented or reduced a fall in such lending when the country's balance of payments difficulties had become especially severe. Banks welcomed an agreement between the Fund and a member because it gave the banks an assurance that the member had undertaken a commitment to follow policies that could be expected to strengthen its balance of payments.

Participants observed that the amount of financial assistance provided by the Fund was often small relative to the size of a country's payments deficit. They suggested that, in such a case, the Fund might be exceeding its terms of reference by asking the country to implement a strong adjustment program. The Fund staff pointed out that a country's payments imbalance could not be measured by the absolute size of its current account deficit but rather by the excess of this deficit over that which the country could finance on terms and conditions that were consistent with its capacity to repay. Nevertheless, it was true that the unsustainable portion of a member's current account deficit was sometimes large in relation to the financial assistance the member could obtain from the Fund. This did not mean, however, that the Fund was exceeding its authority by expecting the member to adopt an adjustment program that was sufficiently strong to solve its balance of payments problem. In fact, it was precisely the availability of relatively limited financial assistance that called for a strong adjustment effort; the lesser the financing, the sterner the adjustment.

It was also noted that Fund members were well aware, through their Executive Directors and from other sources, of the amount of assistance they could obtain from the Fund and the kinds of policy conditions that the Fund was likely to attach to this assistance. With this information, if they did not believe that, on balance, it was advantageous for them to borrow from the Fund, then—being sovereign countries—they did not need to do so. When members sought Fund support, they did so because they believed they would benefit from it. The benefits they expected included assistance from the Fund in formulating and monitoring adjustment programs, financial resources from the Fund, and additional assistance from the international financial community as a result of the agreement with the Fund.

Collaboration Between the Fund and the World Bank

P.R. Narvekar

The Fund and the World Bank are often referred to as twin institutions. They were born at about the same time, and their childhood home was the same—1818 H Street in Washington, D.C. These twin institutions, however, were not expected to look alike, and they have never done so. Nevertheless, their relationship is perhaps closer than that of any other two international organizations.

The Fund and the Bank rely on each other to function effectively. The founding fathers of the two institutions fully recognized that the Bank needed the Fund; they provided that only members of the Fund could become members of the Bank. It is important that members of the Bank subscribe to the code of international conduct that was written into the Fund's Articles of Agreement. By the same token, for effective relations with those of its members which are developing countries, the Fund needs the Bank. The success of the Fund in promoting adjustment depends on help from the World Bank, especially in effecting appropriate changes in the allocation of resources—in particular, in the pattern of public and private investment—within national economies.

The World Bank

The World Bank is the foremost institution helping the developing countries to raise their standards of living. The World Bank is in fact not one but a group of three institutions—the International Bank for Reconstruction and Development (IBRD), the International Development Association (IDA), and the International Finance Corporation

(IFC). The IBRD was established along with the Fund. IDA was created in 1960 when it became clear that many poor countries could only afford to borrow on terms that were more concessionary than those offered by the IBRD. IDA was set up as an affiliate of the IBRD, and although the two are legally and technically distinct entities, they operate as a closely integrated unit and are administered by the same staff. Hereinafter, this composite unit will be referred to as the World Bank, or simply the Bank, unless the context clearly implies a different meaning. No further mention will be made of the IFC, with which the Fund has very few ties.

The World Bank promotes the development of the developing countries by channeling resources to them from the developed countries. For the IBRD, these resources are drawn only to a small extent from its own capital. Less than a tenth of the IBRD's authorized capital has been paid in; the rest serves as a guarantee for the IBRD's borrowings, which are its principal source of funds for lending. By mid-1982, the IBRD had borrowed a cumulative total of US$55 billion. These borrowings were from private investors and on commercial terms; the IBRD's lending is therefore also on commercial terms. The rate of interest on IBRD loans was 9.6 percent at mid-1981; the average repayment period has been about 20 years.

IDA's credits are free of interest but entail a 0.75 percent service charge and a 50-year repayment period, repayment beginning after a 10-year grace period. These terms are made possible because IDA's resources are drawn principally from the budgetary contributions of the richer countries. Without such funds, it would be impossible for the World Bank to provide significant help to the poorest of countries. IDA resources are made available only to countries that are below a periodically adjusted "poverty ceiling" defined in terms of per capita income (at present, US$730 per capita); other criteria for eligibility to IDA credits are that a country be faced with unusually difficult balance of payments problems but still enjoy sufficient economic, financial, and political stability and display a genuine commitment to development. More than 70 countries, including China, have been eligible for IDA assistance. Some 25 countries have received only IDA credits; some 50 have received a "blend" of IDA credits and IBRD loans.

Total World Bank (IBRD plus IDA) lending has increased from an annual average of US$3.8 billion during 1971–75 to US$9.3 billion in

1976–81 and to US$13.0 billion in fiscal year 1982. The World Bank draws up a five-year lending program for each country, which is revised annually. The program is based on specific projects agreed on with the national government. Under the Bank's charter, its lending must be primarily for specific projects. Loans for sectors and to intermediary institutions, however, are permissible. About a third of the lending in 1981 was for agricultural and rural development projects, about a sixth for energy projects, and about a tenth each for transportation projects and development finance companies. The principal change over the years has been a sharp reduction in the proportion of lending going to transportation and a largely offsetting increase in that going to agriculture and rural development. About 40 percent of total World Bank lending in the past ten years or so has been allocated to Asian countries.

Only in "special circumstances" is the World Bank allowed by its charter to lend for nonproject purposes. The Bank's principal objective of bringing about transfers of resources from the developed to the developing countries can be attained through project lending. Such lending, however, is not flexible enough to secure quickly an increase in the rate of such transfers to any particular country should such a need arise. Nonproject lending is undertaken when unforeseen temporary difficulties facing a country give rise to an immediate need for foreign exchange, without which normal development activity would be adversely affected. To obtain such lending, a country must have an acceptable medium-term or long-term development program. It should also pursue policies that would make it possible for normal development activity to eventually resume without such special assistance. Because such lending is considered appropriate only under special circumstances, its scope has been limited. Except in the early postwar reconstruction years, lending of this nature has generally constituted less than 10 percent of the Bank's total lending; during 1970–80, it averaged only 5 percent a year.

In April 1980, the Bank inaugurated a new policy called "structural adjustment lending." This initiative was taken when the Bank saw that the economic problems faced by developing countries were greatly exacerbated by an unfavorable international economic environment—the oil price increases, the increases in interest rates, and stagflation in the developed countries. The developing countries need to adjust the structure of their economies if they are to cope adequately with this unfavorable environment without impairing their growth. While the rate of growth of output in these economies has to be sustained in the face of the new difficulties, the composition of output growth has to be changed so that exports can grow faster and imports slower than would otherwise occur. Policy and institutional changes are also necessary. Under the structural adjustment lending policy, the World Bank has stepped in to help countries draw up and implement the policy reforms needed for this purpose and to provide financial assistance while the structural adjustment takes place. This is necessarily a long process, and for this reason, three or four structural adjustment loans over a period of five or six years are envisaged for each country in which the Bank has negotiated a structural adjustment lending program. The structural adjustment programs supported by the Bank have covered a wide range of economic policies and institutional arrangements relating to these policies. Of course, only those aspects of policy which are considered relevant in a particular case are covered in each structural adjustment loan. In the two and a half years since the inauguration of the structural adjustment lending policy, 17 operations have been completed in 13 countries, including 4 Asian countries (Korea, Pakistan, the Philippines, and Thailand). The 17 operations have involved total commitments of about US$2.2 billion. In the fiscal year ended June 30, 1982, structural adjustment loan commitments represented about 10 percent of total Bank lending.

It is crucial to note that the Bank's lending also has other, nonfinancial, goals. In the context of its lending, the Bank advises borrowing countries on the best way of attaining their development objectives. It engages in a continuous dialogue with the borrowing countries concerning their policies at the project, sector, and macroeconomic levels. In deciding on its lending to a country, the Bank takes into account the country's performance in a variety of areas relating to the development process. Although the scope of such policy dialogue and performance appraisal is limited when the Bank's involvement is confined to project lending, it can be very broad indeed when structural adjustment lending is involved. Thus, the Bank has its own "conditionality," and the need for coordinating it with that of the Fund is evident.

A Brief History of Fund-Bank Relations[1]

During the negotiations that culminated in the Bretton Woods Agreement, the establishment of a single organization performing the functions now assigned to the Fund and the Bank had been considered. This idea was rejected, however, because it was not considered feasible for a single organization to perform effectively all the functions that were to be entrusted to the two. There was also a risk of overcentralization of power and a danger of making costly errors of judgment. The Fund and the Bank were thus established as two independent organizations with separate responsibilities as well as different purposes and functions. In broad terms, the Fund was designed to promote international monetary cooperation and, thus, to facilitate the adjustment of external payments imbalances of its members, and the Bank was designed to help reconstruct economies damaged by the war and to further the longer-term growth and development of developing countries.

While these purposes are distinct, they are also complementary and, in some areas, overlapping. It had always been recognized, therefore, that the two institutions would rely on each other for advice and guidance in each other's areas of primary responsibility. No attempt was made, however, to formally delineate the scope of operations of each institution. The Fund and the Bank were expected to collaborate closely and to draw on each other's expertise; this expertise was to develop as each institution sought to accomplish its own purpose. No organizational mechanism was created to coordinate the two institutions. Nor has any such mechanism been developed since then. The Executive Boards, the managements, and the staff of the two are completely independent of each other.[2] Cooperation between the institutions has thus been based on the capacity of the two staffs to draw on each other's help when assisting their members.

---

[1]For an excellent account of the development of Fund-Bank relations, see Joseph Gold, "The Relationship Between the International Monetary Fund and the World Bank," *Creighton Law Review*, Creighton University School of Law, Vol. 15, No. 2 (1982), pp. 499–521.

[2]There are cases, however, in which the same person represents a country in the Executive Boards of both the Fund and the Bank—the so-called dual Executive Directors.

When the two institutions expanded their operations in the developing countries in the 1950s and early 1960s, there was an increasing need to promote cooperation between the two staffs and to minimize the risk of duplication of effort, which in certain instances could lead to inconsistent or even contradictory policy advice to member countries. To facilitate this process, a set of guidelines was issued by the two managements to their respective Executive Boards in February 1966, specifying for the first time the procedures for this cooperation.

In December 1966, as a result of discussions following the Board's approval of these guidelines, the Managing Director of the Fund issued a "Memorandum on Fund-Bank Collaboration" to the department heads of the Fund. The Bank was "recognized as having primary responsibility for the composition and appropriateness of development programs and project evaluation, including development priorities." The Fund was "recognized as having primary responsibility for exchange rates and restrictive systems, for adjustment of temporary balance of payments disequilibria and for evaluating and assisting members to work out stabilization programs as a sound basis for economic advance." These broad distinctions were not intended to preclude discussions between the two staffs on matters that were within the area of primary responsibility of one or the other institution; they did indicate, however, that the staff of each institution was required to inform itself of the established views and positions of the other in those areas where the other institution was primarily responsible and to "adopt those views as a working basis for their own work" and not to "engage in a critical review of those matters with member countries unless it is done with the prior consent" of the other institution.

The guidelines also recognized that "in between these two clear-cut areas of responsibility of the Bank and the Fund, respectively, there is the broad range of matters which are of interest to both institutions. . . . In connection with all such matters, efforts should be made to avoid conflicting views and judgments, through continuing close working relations between the respective area departments and other means."

The question of Fund-Bank cooperation was reviewed again by the managements of the two institutions in 1970, and a detailed set of guidelines relating to the procedural arrangements for cooperation was circulated to the two staffs in a joint memorandum by the Managing Director of the Fund and the President of the Bank. This memorandum affirmed that the 1966 understandings had served the interests of the organizations and their member countries and continued to be valid as the basis for future cooperation.

Since then, because of a number of recent developments, there has been a renewed interest in the effectiveness of cooperation between the Fund and the Bank. The sharp deterioration in the external terms of trade for non-oil developing countries, combined with unfavorable conditions in the world financial and export markets, has resulted in large and structural external imbalances in many developing countries. These imbalances, in turn, have led to greater demand for financial resources from both the Fund and the Bank. The Fund's response, initially under its extended Fund facility established in 1974, has been to provide larger amounts of financing for longer periods and to concentrate more on the supply aspects of the members' economies. The Bank has responded by introducing structural adjustment lending, which, as described earlier, is designed to provide foreign exchange to support the development of the export sector and the import substituting sector in the medium term. As the two institutions have adapted their policies to increase their assistance to members facing large imbalances, they have both moved closer to the edge of their traditional spheres of responsibility and expertise, reinforcing the need for effective cooperation.

Effective collaboration between the Fund and the Bank in respect of a particular country does not require, however, that either or both of the two institutions should lend to that country in a particular form, say, the extended Fund facility in the case of the Fund and structural adjustment lending in the case of the Bank. There have been striking instances of very effective collaboration between the two institutions—to the benefit of member countries—without the existence of either an extended arrangement or a structural adjustment loan. It is important to note that the need for effective collaboration has been heightened by recent world economic developments and by the responses of the Fund and the Bank to these developments.

The two institutions reviewed the effectiveness of their cooperative efforts in mid-1980 and early 1981. This review reaffirmed that there was no need to revise the procedural aspects of cooperation. It did point out, however, that under current circumstances there was a greater need for more direct forms of exchange.

The Fund's Areas of Expertise

The Fund conducts an annual consultation with its members to review their economic development and policies. In this consultation, the Fund staff carries out a thorough assessment of members' macroeconomic policies. As a consequence, it has gained considerable experience in analyzing fiscal, monetary, and incomes policies, exchange rate policies, and foreign trade and external debt policies. This experience has enabled the staff to assist its members in designing stabilization programs aimed at balance of payments adjustment.

An important element of any stabilization program is the formulation of a "financial program," which aims at ensuring consistency between financial policies and the likely balance of payments outcome. For this purpose, a forecast of the demand for money consistent with growth and inflation targets has to be made. The expected increase in the demand for money should match the expected increase in the supply, which is based on the planned increase in supply of credit to the public and private sectors and on the changes in net foreign assets (i.e., the balance of payments target). If the projected figures for both demand and supply of money are not consistent, the planned set of measures affecting the public and the private sectors needs to be reviewed and adjusted. The most difficult problem in this exercise is often the adjustment of fiscal imbalances to a level that does not result in excessive creation of liquidity and, at the same time, does not impinge on the availability of credit to the private sector. Adjustment of budgetary expenditure or the introduction of revenue measures requires a thorough assessment before major policy decisions are made. Complementary monetary measures, including those relating to the efficiency of the financial system in allocating credit and the appropriateness of the levels and structure of interest rates, are an integral part of the financial program.

In many situations of balance of payments difficulty, the Fund has found that an adjustment of the exchange rate is necessary to reduce the demand for imports and to expand the export sector and the import substituting sector. In these cases, the Fund staff has worked closely with the authorities to determine the appropriate extent of the adjustment and the most effective manner of implementing it.

With the emergence of large and structural imbalances in the 1970s, it became apparent that, in many cases, demand management policies such as those mentioned above, even when accompanied by an exchange rate change, were not adequate to bring about the required adjustment of the balance of payments. In cases where large and protracted disequilibria have disrupted the structure of the economy, additional supply-oriented policies are needed to reallocate resources in the economy and to restore external viability. Because such restructuring of production and trade requires a longer adjustment period, the Fund has increasingly provided assistance in support of medium-term adjustment programs with emphasis on supply-oriented policies.

The ultimate objective of a medium-term adjustment program is, of course, to bring the balance of payments into a sustainable position. This involves reducing the current account deficit to a level consistent with the country's capacity to acquire and to service external debt. Consequently, a thorough evaluation of the availability of different kinds of foreign financing—international bank credit, loans from governmental aid agencies and development finance institutions, trade financing from credit/guarantor agencies—has to be undertaken.

The desired adjustment in the current account needs to be addressed in terms of underlying changes in the economy brought about by changes in investment, savings, output, and thus the debt servicing capacity. A country's external debt is sustainable if the available resources are used productively and if the economic rate of return to marginal investment exceeds the cost of foreign financing. Clearly, appropriate demand management policies play an important role in the efficient allocation of resources and are a necessary ingredient of any medium-term adjustment program. In addition, however, attention must be focused on those policies that directly affect the allocation of resources. In many developing countries, the public sector undertakes the bulk of investment and/or administers a variety of prices, in particular producer prices in the export sector. Therefore, in assessing the medium-term adjustment strategy, due emphasis must be given to the appropriateness of the allocation of investment by the public sector and of the structure of relative prices confronting the private sector. It is in this area that the Fund staff needs to rely heavily on the expertise of the Bank staff.

The Bank's Areas of Expertise

The Bank has always recognized that the broad policy framework of a country that the Bank supports through its project loans must be appropriately designed if the country's development objectives are to be reached. Therefore, the Bank undertakes a considerable amount of economic and sector work. About 20 percent of the Bank's operational staff time is devoted to such work. Some of this work simply updates macroeconomic and sector data and reviews broad development issues. Other work analyzes the specific development issues and the obstacles to growth and development in a given country. Policy and institutional reforms that are required are then defined. The distinguishing feature of the Bank's work—in areas in which it overlaps with work done in the Fund—is its longer-term focus, which involves a large amount of detailed sectoral work.

The specific projects financed by the Bank are evaluated by the Bank's sectoral experts. In evaluating the feasibility of specific projects, the Bank staff carefully assesses not only the economics of the project itself but also the appropriateness of the policies of the country concerned relating to the sector to which the project belongs. Consequently, through the normal course of its lending operations, the Bank has accumulated substantial information on the microeconomic aspects of its members' economies.

> The World Bank's elaborate project supervision system, which covers all Bank-assisted projects under execution and is supplemented by findings of country economic and sector work performed within the organization, has long been the principal means for the Bank to learn from its operating experience. The supervision system consists of regular reporting by the borrowers, periodic field visits by Bank staff, regular middle management reviews of progress in solving implementation problems, a semiannual review by senior management of the status of the more serious problem projects, and an annual general discussion of problems in project implementation.[3]

On the basis of the extensive information compiled and analyzed by its sectoral experts, the Bank is in a position to assess member countries' sectoral policies that embrace microeconomic decisions on pricing, taxation, and subsidization of specific products. Pricing,

---

[3]World Bank, *Operations Evaluation: World Bank Standards and Procedures*, 2nd edition (Washington, August 1979), p. 10.

taxation, and subsidy policies have a direct impact on cost-profitability relationships in various sectors of the economy and, thereby, on the efficient allocation of resources. A typical experience in developing countries is that pricing, taxation, and subsidy policies that are designed to benefit consumers have resulted in lowered production incentives—and thus in supply shortages—or in inefficient use of essential inputs, such as fertilizer, water, or energy products, in the production process.

The allocative impact of pricing, taxation, and subsidy policies is particularly important in those cases where public enterprises that are subject to these policies play a dominant role in the economy. In such cases, pricing, taxation, and subsidy policies can have pervasive macroeconomic effects because they directly affect the financial position of the public enterprises concerned. Inappropriate policies can lead to large public sector deficits and more rapid expansion of domestic credit. The Bank, however, has generally focused on the allocative aspect of pricing and subsidy policies, while the Fund has concentrated on the broader macroeconomic impact of these policies on the budgetary and the balance of payments positions.

Because of the Bank's extensive sectoral work in many countries, it is in an excellent position to evaluate their overall investment priorities consistent with their long-term development strategy. The wide-ranging expertise of the Bank staff places it in a unique position to assist countries in analyzing various aspects of their public investment programs and to offer advice on development priorities with respect to size and composition of the programs, recurrent outlays necessary to support the programs, and the efficiency of resource use. A prime objective of the Bank is to assist countries to develop the institutional framework necessary to improve their capacity for determining sectoral priorities and criteria for project evaluation, establishing and implementing public investment programs, and reviewing investment plans and government budgets.

Areas of Common Interest

It is clear that, in spite of their distinct purposes and functions, there are large areas where the interests of the Fund and the Bank overlap. This is natural since most economies are sufficiently integrated that any policy or development that affects one part or aspect of an economy is certain to affect large segments of the rest. Besides this commonality of interests in a general sense, the Fund and the Bank share an interest in a number of specific areas. The 1966 guidelines for Fund-Bank collaboration recognized that "there is the broad range of matters which is of interest to both institutions. This range includes such matters as the structure and functioning of financial institutions, the adequacy of money and capital markets, the actual and potential capacity of a member country to generate domestic savings, the financial implications of economic development programs both for the internal financial position of a country and for its external situation, foreign debt problems, and so on."

In all these areas, close working relations have been established between the Fund and the Bank staff so as to avoid duplication of effort. For example, both institutions are interested in technical assistance in the fiscal field, particularly in the field of tax policy and fiscal administration. In practice, however, the Bank does not offer technical assistance in this area and relies on the Fiscal Affairs Department of the Fund, which provides this assistance on behalf of both institutions. Under this arrangement, regular meetings are held and information is exchanged between the Fiscal Affairs Department of the Fund and the Economics Department of the Bank to ensure that fiscal experts address issues of concern to both organizations.

Both the Fund and the Bank are also keenly interested in the issue of external debt because debt problems are generally a manifestation of underlying balance of payments difficulties, which often require structural adjustment of the economy through appropriate macroeconomic and microeconomic policies. The two institutions have worked closely in this area by analyzing various aspects of the external indebtedness of countries. The Fund focuses on short-term economic and financial policies, prospects, and requirements in cases where external debt difficulties are acute. The Bank concentrates its attention on long-term borrowing, development strategy, and debt management. Both the Fund and the Bank are represented at meetings of multilateral debt renegotiations carried out under the auspices of "creditor clubs" (e.g., the Paris Club).

The Executive Board of the Fund has recently approved proposals for the Fund's role in future debt renegotiation exercises. Under these proposals:

The Fund and the Bank would continue to cooperate closely within the framework of existing arrangements; specifically, the Fund would continue to avail itself of the Bank's extensive data on debt, while it is expected that the Bank would have access to Fund information on balance of payments and short-term debt. To the extent that the analysis to be undertaken must include assessments bearing on policies and prospects of a developmental or long-term nature, it would be expected that the Bank would provide a separate report on these aspects for the participants. If the Bank were approached by a debtor country for an assessment of its economic situation and prospects, the Fund staff would stand ready to cooperate with the Bank staff by providing information and analysis on matters within the Fund's competence.[4]

Operational Aspects of Fund-Bank Cooperation

The substantive purpose of Fund-Bank collaboration is to improve the effectiveness of each institution in assisting member countries to design appropriate programs of adjustment and development. In principle, the ideal situation from an institutional and operational point of view would be one in which the Bank was responsible for the design and monitoring of the investment plan and pricing policies of a country and the Fund for its balance of payments adjustment policies. These two aspects of adjustment could then be combined to form a comprehensive adjustment program. In reality, the situation is much more complicated. Two types of complication arise: one relating to the limitations on the ability of each institution to provide the other with the required input; and the other relating to the practical difficulties of incorporating this input into the specific adjustment programs supported by each institution.

In general, the Fund and the Bank rely extensively on the information exchanged through informal contacts between the staffs as well as that contained in their respective reports. When one institution receives information or data from a country on a confidential basis, this confidentiality is, of course, fully respected. An effective means of utilizing the expertise of the other institution has been to include staff members in each other's missions, subject to the consent of the country concerned. In recent years, the number of missions including staff from the other organization has increased considerably. For example, the Bank participated in a recent Fund staff mission to China. There is

---

[4]Bahram Nowzad, Richard C. Williams, and others, *External Indebtedness of Developing Countries*, IMF Occasional Paper No. 3 (Washington, May 1981), p. 29.

limited scope, however, for expanding this form of cooperation because of the severe manpower constraints faced by both institutions.

Aside from these constraints, the ability of each institution to assist the other depends largely on its level of involvement in the specific country concerned. By the nature of its operations, the Fund tends to be closely involved in the assessment of financial policies of all its members on a more or less regular basis. The Bank provides financial and technical assistance in different sectors of the economy and for a wide range of projects. The level of Bank involvement in specific countries is dictated by limitations of financial and human resources and by the priorities it sets regarding the relative importance of a member's needs; the Bank tends to be more selective in its involvement with its members. Consequently, it may sometimes be difficult to coordinate the operations of the two institutions in cases in which they may have different priorities.

A related issue is the difference in the operational time horizons of the Fund and the Bank. In many cases, by the time a member approaches the Fund, its economic and financial position has already deteriorated to a critical stage. To avoid further deteriorioation, appropriate policies need to be implemented fairly quickly. Therefore, Fund-supported programs are often negotiated in a somewhat short period, and Fund missions operate on a tight schedule.

By contrast, the Bank's task of evaluating members' investment and pricing policies is a time-consuming process because it involves a coordinated analysis of various sectors of the economy. There is a great deal of information available in the Bank relating to specific sectors of the economy. Compiling all the information on specific projects and sectors in order to ascertain their implications for the broader developmental aspects of a member's economy, such as the appropriate investment strategy, is an exercise that takes time. Even more difficult is the task of converting the generalizations derived from diagnostic studies into specific policy recommendations that can be dovetailed into the decision-making process of member countries. Another element affecting the time horizon of the Bank's work is that a prime objective of the Bank is to assist its member countries in building up local capacity to carry out work in key areas. For example, rather than assessing an investment program itself, the Bank will sometimes help a country to develop its own capacity to perform appraisals. Although the latter is more time-consuming, the Bank considers that, in some cases, this use of its manpower is more efficient.

In assessing a country's adjustment program, the Fund and the Bank must each rely on the input of the other. Both institutions, however, are careful to avoid attaching additional criteria to their lending that would delay or reduce the flow of resources to the country. In their recent review of Fund-Bank cooperation, both institutions have emphasized that closer relations between their two staffs should not lead to any "cross-conditionality"—that is, when a country is required to satisfy policy prescriptions by one institution in order to secure a financial arrangement with the other. Each institution should retain its separate functions and full responsibility for its own decisions. The purpose of cooperation is to increase the knowledge on the basis of which such decisions are made and to improve the effectiveness of the assistance provided to members. The purpose is not to achieve bureaucratic cohesiveness between the two institutions. In the final analysis, it is the institution with which the member concludes a financial arrangement that must decide whether a country's policies are adequate.

In practice, the extent of each institution's involvement in providing the other with an input for assessing a country's adjustment program depends on the scope of the particular program. For instance, in some Fund-supported programs, where the involvement of the public sector in the investment program is not very important, a Bank assessment of the program would not be essential. In those cases, however, where the appropriateness of the public investment program is crucial to the success of the adjustment effort, the Fund obviously needs to take into account the views of the Bank before entering into a financial arrangement. In some cases, the Bank may not be in a position to provide a detailed assessment of the investment program but may be able to indicate whether the general thrust of the program is in the right direction, making it possible for the Fund to proceed with an arrangement without waiting for a detailed Bank assessment. In yet other cases, the public investment program may be dominated by a few large projects, such as hydroelectric or public works projects. In such cases, before entering into an arrangement, the Fund must have an indication from the Bank's sectoral experts that this heavy investment is justified and properly phased.

The focus of the Bank's structural adjustment programs is on the appropriate size and composition of the country's public investment program, on the need to improve the efficiency of enterprises in the public sector, and on policy changes in the agricultural, industrial, and energy sectors. The success of any such medium-term program, however, depends greatly on the appropriateness of domestic financial and exchange rate policies. In a fundamental sense, a medium-term program can be viewed as a succession of short-term programs. It is, therefore, essential that a member's short-term financial policies be consistent with its long-term developmental goals and that the Bank take into account the views of the Fund on the member's general financial situation and policies before concluding a medium-term structural adjustment loan. For instance, in cases where a country's structural adjustment program requires a medium-term target for the current account of the balance of payments, the Bank looks to the Fund to develop such a target in close consultation with the national authorities. The Bank also seeks the judgment of the Fund on exchange rate policy issues. This does not mean that the Bank staff cannot or does not have views on exchange rate policy; they do, and the Fund staff takes those views into account in forming its own judgment. As indicated earlier, however, this is an example of an area where the ultimate responsibility rests with one institution.

*   *   *

In conclusion, close cooperation between the Fund and the Bank is an essential ingredient of the continuing effort to improve the effectiveness of the assistance each institution provides its members. The two institutions play a central role in facilitating the financing and adjustment of the structural imbalances faced by many developing countries. Under the current difficult world economic conditions, it is ever more important for the two institutions to work closely together and complement each other's policy advice to member countries. By combining their expertise in various aspects of economic policy, the Fund and the Bank can greatly enhance the impact of their financial assistance on member countries.

Summary of Discussion

The discussion covered a wide range of subjects relating to both the Bank and the Fund, including the possibility of conflict between the two organizations when they borrowed funds, their attitudes toward the freezing of foreign-owned assets by some members, and the barriers preventing citizens of developing countries from heading the two organizations. The nature and functions of creditor clubs and the role that the Fund could play in promoting the North-South dialogue were also discussed.

Participants observed that neither the Bank nor the Fund had financed its lending activities wholly from capital subscriptions. The substantial borrowing needs of the two organizations in fact created considerable potential for conflict between them when they sought funds. The Fund staff pointed out that no conflicts had arisen in the commercial markets because the Fund had not yet borrowed in these markets.

References were made to recent instances where countries had frozen assets that were under their control but were owned by residents of other countries. Participants were interested in how the Bank and the Fund viewed these measures. The Fund staff pointed out that such actions were not of direct concern to the Bank. Nor, to the extent that assets were frozen for security reasons, were such measures within the purview of the Fund. In other cases, however, the measures conflicted with the Fund's code of conduct, and the member introducing them was expected to consult with the Fund on the manner and timing of their removal.

Since 1946, when the first President of the Bank and the first Managing Director of the Fund were elected, a citizen of the United States had headed the Bank and a European had headed the Fund. Participants inquired about the reasons for this, noting that membership in the two organizations had increased substantially and the relative economic importance of different regional groupings had changed considerably during the last 36 years. In particular, they wanted to know whether there were any formal barriers that prevented a citizen of a developing country from heading either the Bank or the Fund.

The Fund staff observed that, when the Board of Governors of the Fund held its Inaugural Meeting in Savannah, Georgia, in March 1946, it had been widely expected that the United States would nominate Harry Dexter White, a U.S. citizen who was also one of the chief architects of the Fund, to be the first Managing Director. The U.S. authorities, however, apparently believed that it was more important for the President of the Bank to be a U.S. citizen, so that the Bank would be accepted in the international capital markets, which at the time were dominated by the New York market. They also believed that it would not be appropriate for U.S. citizens to head both organizations. Accordingly, Eugene Meyer, from the United States, became the first President of the Bank, and Camille Gutt, a citizen of Belgium, was elected to be the first Managing Director of the Fund. The Fund staff added that there were no legal barriers that might prevent citizens of other member countries from heading the Bank or the Fund.

Participants commented on the sharp increase in the number of countries experiencing payments arrears, on the prospective need for some of these countries to seek rescheduling of their debts, and on the role played by creditor clubs in debt rescheduling exercises. With respect to the last, the Fund staff noted that the creditor clubs were informal gatherings of government officials from both creditor countries and the debtor country concerned. Their purpose was to help countries experiencing debt servicing difficulties to cope with them in an orderly manner. The best-known creditor club was the Paris Club, but others, such as the London Club and the Hague Club, were also important. The Paris Club, which had explicit rules and procedures, handled reschedulings of official credits. The other clubs were less formal and dealt with reschedulings of private debt, including debt owed to commercial banks.

Participants observed that the North-South dialogue appeared to have reached a stalemate and that this was having an adverse effect on relations between the developing and the industrial countries. An important reason for the stalemate was the different views that the two groups of countries held about equity. Countries from the South took an international view and believed that the goal of equity should be structural reform of the international monetary system. On the other hand, countries from the North took an individual approach and claimed that the goal should be reasonable equality of incomes among individuals; therefore, they argued, aid should contribute to the satisfaction of basic human needs. It was suggested that the Bank and the Fund should attempt to reconcile these views and do whatever else was in their power to accelerate progress on the dialogue.

The Fund staff agreed that countries from the North and the South tended to have different perceptions of equity. The countries of the North strongly rejected the international approach. They were concerned that the revenue collected from their own taxpayers, including middle-income and lower-income taxpayers, be used to meet the basic needs of the poor, not merely the wants of the rich in the countries that were recipients of aid.

Many of the developing countries claimed that the approach of the industrial countries was hypocritical insofar as it was used to justify a smaller commitment or slower disbursement of aid. They argued that donor countries could always give aid in such a manner that it would benefit primarily the poor in the developing countries. The developing countries also argued that the rich countries had little real understanding of class relations in the poor countries and that, by focusing so much attention on the end-uses of their aid, the rich countries were interfering unduly with the social structures of developing countries.

The Fund staff noted that the Bank and the Fund were intergovernmental, not supranational, institutions. Their scope for action was determined by their members. They could not remove the political barriers to progress in the North-South dialogue. What they could do was provide analyses, where requested, of proposals in their own areas of competence. These analyses could facilitate progress by throwing light on the implications of different courses of action and by helping to focus attention on areas where useful compromises could be made.

The SDR—An Introduction

Wm. C. Hood*

My comments on the SDR will be in three parts: the origin of the SDR, the nature of the SDR, and the future of the SDR.

The Origin of the SDR

The SDR originated in the late 1960s during the period of fixed exchange rates. Monetary authorities held reserves that could be used to maintain the external value of their currencies in foreign exchange markets. Thus, for example, if the United Kingdom held U.S. dollars in its reserves, and if the demand for the pound sterling were to fall and therefore the value of the pound were also to fall in the market, the U.K. authorities could use their dollars to buy pounds and thus stop the decline in the value of the pound. Similarly, if the demand for pounds should be strong and the value of the pound should start to rise, the U.K. authorities could sell pounds for dollars. In that case, the amount of dollars in their reserves would be increased.

As a matter of practice, countries held their official reserves mainly in the form of gold and U.S. dollars. Their "working reserves" were dollars. This was natural because the dollar was the principal form of money used in international transactions. Of course, some countries held pounds or deutsche mark in their reserves because it was more appropriate for them given their trading patterns.

The formal link between U.S. dollar reserves and gold reserves was maintained by the willingness of the U.S. authorities to exchange gold

---

*This paper, a brief introduction to the SDR, was delivered by Mr. Hood as Mr. R.J. Familton, the scheduled speaker on the subject of SDRs, was unable to attend the colloquium. Mr. Familton's paper was distributed to the participants and appears in this volume beginning on page 146.

and dollars at a fixed rate. This system, by which dollars linked to gold served as reserves, was known as the gold exchange standard.

The U.S. dollar was a good reserve asset because it satisfied the principal requirements of a good money: It served as a unit of account, as a store of value, and as a medium of exchange. As a unit of account, it was a useful measure of value because it was widely used in the world, both in official and in commercial transactions. As a store of value, it was as good as any other asset because of its link to gold. As a medium of exchange, it was outstanding because (1) it was generally acceptable by other monetary authorities; (2) it was usable in dealings with commercial banks in the foreign exchange markets; and (3) the large capital market of the United States was available to serve the credit needs of official entities seeking to borrow reserves.

But problems arose with the gold exchange standard. In a growing world economy, there is a growing demand for reserves. But two contradictions, or asymmetries, in the system impaired its ability to supply reserves:

First, even if the supply of dollars could be expanded, the gold backing for the U.S. dollar could not be expanded, or at least not smoothly. So, as more dollars were backed by the same gold stock, or even a smaller gold stock in the United States, the convertibility of the dollar became doubtful, and the U.S. dollar itself became less acceptable.

Second, the asymmetry of the system whereby one country could draw resources from the rest of the world through a current account deficit and pay for them by issuing reserves seemed inequitable and therefore unacceptable.

Therefore, the search began for a resolution of the contradictions. Over the years, several approaches have been considered and tried, and the quest still continues.

One idea that was considered and rejected was that, if the physical supply of gold could not be controlled—being subject to the uncertainties of new gold discoveries and to changes in industrial demands—perhaps the value of gold in the system could be increased by raising the price of gold. There were many reasons for rejecting this idea. An important reason was that, because of the distribution of gold holdings, the gains from the increase in the gold price would be inequitably distributed.

Another idea for resolving the contradictions that has proved to be ineffective was the idea that, if the supply of reserves could not grow to meet the demand, perhaps the demand itself could be reduced. It was thought by some that, if the world moved to floating exchange rates, monetary authorities would no longer need or wish to hold reserves. But our experience with the floating rate system has now proved that this view was incorrect. Even with floating exchange rates, monetary authorities still wish to hold reserves in growing amounts.

Creating a new reserve asset was yet another idea. It was felt that, if a new reserve asset were created by a group of countries, and best of all by the Fund itself, it would resolve the inequity implied by the then existing system that concentrated the reserve-creating power mainly in the United States. And so the idea of a new reserve asset, issued by the Fund and serving as a supplement to gold, was born. The Articles of Agreement of the Fund were amended, with effect from July 28, 1969, to authorize the Fund to allocate SDRs to its members, in proportion to their quotas, in order "to meet the need, as and when it arises, for a supplement to existing reserve assets."

The Articles provide that decisions to allocate SDRs shall be taken for so-called basic periods of up to five years in duration. In the first basic period 1970–72, SDR 9.3 billion was allocated; in the second basic period 1973–77, no SDRs were allocated; and in the third basic period 1978–81, SDR 12.0 billion was allocated. No decision to allocate SDRs in the fourth basic period has yet been taken, and SDR 21.3 billion is outstanding.

It was hoped that the SDR might become the principal reserve asset of the system. Manifestly, it has not yet done so, although one day it may. But the world has been exploring other resolutions of the gold exchange standard contradictions while continuing to experiment with the SDR.

Another approach to the contradictions was to abandon the formal link to gold. In 1971, the United States withdrew its undertaking to meet official demands to convert U.S. dollars to gold. This action resolved one of the contradictions but not the other, namely, the asymmetry in the distribution of reserve-issuing power.

For a while, the world responded to this asymmetry by diversifying its reserve holdings among currencies. The deutsche mark and, to a lesser extent, the Japanese yen emerged as new reserve currencies. The pound sterling has been a reserve currency for a long time. The

Europeans created a new composite unit—the European Currency Unit—which, for members of the European Monetary System, serves as one form of reserve holding.

During this period when countries were diversifying their reserves among currencies, much consideration was given in the Fund to the setting up of a substitution account to permit monetary authorities to substitute SDRs for some of their dollar holdings in reserves. Several forms of a substitution account have been considered. The most recent version envisaged that a new account would be opened in the Fund, on one or more specific occasions, to enable members on a prescribed basis to exchange dollars for a form of SDRs. However, interest in the substitution account declined before it could be established—for the same reason that interest in diversifying reserve holdings among currencies declined; namely, the value of the U.S. dollar began once again to appreciate in exchange markets, and therefore the monetary authorities were more content to hold it.

The SDR has not yet become the principal reserve asset. The world continues to need reserves, and it continues to experiment with its reserve system.

Many changes have been made in the characteristics of the SDR since it first came into existence. Instead of listing these changes in detail, I will state the main characteristics of the SDR as it exists today.

The Nature of the SDR

The SDR consists of a credit established in the books of the Special Drawing Rights Department of the Fund in favor of the member. As mentioned above, these credits are created on the occasion of an allocation and are provided in proportion to members' quotas.

The SDR is now defined in terms of a basket, or collection, of the five major currencies of the world: the U.S. dollar, the deutsche mark, the Japanese yen, the French franc, and the pound sterling. The amount of each currency in the basket is fixed for extended periods. The value of the SDR at any time in terms of a given currency may be calculated by using the exchange rates of the constituent currencies against the dollar and the rate of the given currency against the dollar.

Interest is earned and paid on SDRs at a rate calculated quarterly as the weighted average of interest rates on short-term domestic obligations in the five countries whose currencies are included in the SDR basket. The Fund pays interest at this rate to holders of SDRs, and members pay interest to the Fund at this rate on their allocations of SDRs. Thus, a member that holds SDRs in amounts equal to its allocation receives exactly as much interest as it pays. Accordingly, it has, in effect, a costless line of credit. When a member uses its SDRs by exchanging them for currency or settling obligations to the Fund, it draws on this line of credit, and it makes a net interest payment to the Fund on the amount of SDRs used.

Let us look at the present-day SDR in terms of its characteristics as money:

(1) As a unit of account it is easily used, and to date its major use has been as a unit of account. The Fund's accounts are kept exclusively in SDRs. Some 15 international organizations use the SDR as their unit of account or as the basis of their accounting unit. The SDR is also used as a standard of value in a significant number of international conventions such as the Universal Postal Union and the Convention on the Carriage of Goods by Sea. Sixteen members of the Fund peg their exchange rates to the SDR.

(2) As a store of value, the performance of the SDR rests on the performance of its constituent currencies. If the constituent currencies lose their purchasing power at high or uneven rates, the SDR will be less attractive as a store of value than the superior performers among national currencies.

(3) As a medium of exchange, the SDR has as yet only a limited role. This is partly because of the constraints that the Fund puts on the use of the SDR accounts held with it. It is also partly due to the fact that the use of SDR-denominated assets and liabilities by institutions other than the Fund and the monetary authorities that deal with the Fund has so far developed only to a very limited extent.

What uses can be made of SDRs in exchange? They may be used in transactions with the Fund, with other members of the Fund, and with so-called prescribed holders. In transactions with the Fund, members may use SDRs in most instances and must use them in some cases. Charges for the use of Fund resources must be paid in SDRs, and normally a portion of a quota subscription must also be paid in SDRs. Repayment of debts and other transfers to the Fund may be made in SDRs. The Fund, for its part, may make transfers to members in SDRs.

Members of the Fund may use SDRs in a wide variety of official transactions with other members. Thus, they may use SDRs to obtain currency, to extend loans, to make donations, to settle financial obligations, and in other ways.

Members may receive SDRs from other members either by agreement or by designation. In the case of designation, the Fund designates members having an adequately strong international financial position to receive SDRs. Designated members are required to accept SDRs until their holdings reach a figure three times their cumulative allocations.

Prescribed holders are 13 international financial institutions, such as the World Bank and the Bank for International Settlements, and some development banks, which have been authorized by the Fund to deal in SDRs with members of the Fund and institutions having prescribed holder status.

It should be noted that the SDRs allocated by the Fund may only be used in official transactions and then with some restrictions. They cannot be used by official entities in transactions with nonofficial entities such as commercial banks. In this respect, they are quite unlike U.S. dollars.

It is possible for commercial banks and others to issue liabilities and acquire assets denominated in a basket of currencies equivalent to the SDR. To a very limited extent this has happened. It would, in my opinion, have to happen on a very considerable scale if the SDR is to become the principal reserve asset of the system.

The Future of the SDR

The future of the SDR depends partly on actions that the Fund itself may take and partly on the nature of the evolution of the international monetary system at large.

Actions that the Fund may take are of three kinds:

(1) It may improve further some of the technical characteristics of the SDR and of the facilities for its use provided by the Fund. In the last decade, a great many improvements in the original design of the SDR have been made. These have greatly enhanced its acceptability in competition with other official reserve assets and have improved its usability. There is a limited range of further improvements that can be suggested, and the staff of the Fund is studying them and will

probably put some of them to the Executive Board for consideration from time to time. These past and prospective improvements are discussed in some detail in Mr. Familton's paper.

(2) The Fund may resume allocations of SDRs as conditions warrant.

(3) The third kind of action the Fund could take would involve an enlargement of the functions of the SDR in the Fund.

I am now going to refer to some ideas that do not have the approval of the Fund but are simply suggestions that have been put forward in various quarters for discussion.

The Fund could make adjustments in the manner in which it performs its functions so as to accord a larger role to the SDR and a smaller role to currencies in its activities. The advantage that might be derived in making these adjustments would lie in promoting wider use of the SDR as an international asset.

I offer one example simply by way of illustration. The Fund now finances its loans to members mainly by the use of currencies given to the Fund in payment of quota subscriptions. One could, in principle, dispense with this use of currencies. One could retain the concept of the quota to determine voting power and the limits to each member's access to Fund resources. But instead of a member drawing currencies from the Fund when it uses the Fund's facilities, it might very well draw SDRs created specifically for the purpose. These SDRs would then be used in transactions with other members to obtain currencies needed.

As the system evolves, if privately issued SDRs become more commonly used, the Fund might usefully provide accounts through which national central banks could settle SDR-denominated obligations with each other. This technique of settlement would be similar to the arrangements provided by central banks for settlements among commercial banks. This is a Fund service which is by no means required today, but which the Fund might consider offering if it were needed in the future.

The ultimate role of the SDR in the system lies beyond the power of the Fund to determine in any direct or deliberate way. It depends on the evolution of the international monetary system itself. A more integrated system will evolve in a more stable world. A more integrated system will minimize the differences among national currencies and the values of national currencies. In these circumstances, it will be more natural to use composite currency units. When such units are more commonly used in international commerce, they will more naturally be held as official reserves. It is in that kind of integrated world economy that the SDR will come into its own as the principal reserve asset.

The SDR—Its Evolution and Prospects

R.J. Familton

On January 1, 1970, the Fund made the first allocation of special drawing rights (SDRs) to 104 member countries that had become participants in the Special Drawing Account. The allocation marked the culmination of long efforts by many persons—academics, national officials, Fund management and staff, and members of the Fund's Executive Board and of its Board of Governors—to deal with a major weakness in the international monetary system. It also marked the operational beginning of an important new element in the system.

The Period Prior to 1970

The events, studies, discussions, and negotiations that led to the first allocation of SDRs are well documented and need not be repeated here. It is useful, however, to consider one major question—namely, what were the circumstances that prompted the members of the Fund to conclude in the second half of the 1960s that there was a weakness in the international monetary system that required the deliberate creation of international liquidity in the form of the SDR?

As international trade and payments grew in the immediate postwar period, international reserves also expanded, principally through the accumulation of U.S. dollars by official holders. However, toward the end of the 1950s, there was some concern about the future adequacy of international reserves. In the early 1960s, this concern became more widespread as signs of stress in the international monetary system began to multiply. Fears that confidence would not be maintained in reserve media—notably gold and the main currencies used in international transactions, such as the U.S. dollar and the pound sterling—and that the reserve media would fail to grow satisfactorily in line with the growth in the volume of international trade and

146

payments led to intensified discussion and study, both in the Fund and in various groups, on international liquidity, the functioning of the international monetary system, and the role of the Fund.

Following the amendment of the Articles of Agreement with effect from July 28, 1969, the Managing Director's proposal to allocate SDRs for the first basic period was adopted by the Board of Governors on October 3, 1969. The proposal provided for the creation of approximately SDR 9.5 billion during 1970–72.

In this context, several observations made in the Managing Director's proposal are of particular interest:

(1) World reserves, consisting of official holdings of gold, foreign exchange, and reserve positions in the Fund, had declined by more than 50 percent relative to world trade since the early 1950s; relative to international transactions, the decline was even steeper.

(2) From about 1964, there was a change in the situation, which was described in the proposal as follows: ". . . growth of reserves flattened markedly, the ratio of reserves to trade declined more rapidly, the transfer of reserves from deficit to surplus countries ceased to act as a force tending to equalize reserve ratios, and there was increasing resort to international credit as a means of relieving the tightness of reserves."

(3) After taking into consideration the relationship of reserves to the adjustment process (i.e., the correction of payments maladjustments without resort to measures destructive of national or international prosperity), the Managing Director concluded that in the circumstances "the supplementation of reserves would be most unlikely, on balance, to exercise any adverse effect upon the adjustment process, and indeed if nothing were done to supplement reserves the stabilization efforts now being made by deficit countries might well be frustrated by the defensive measures of others."

(4) Although the amended Articles envisaged that decisions of the Fund to allocate SDRs shall normally be for basic periods of five years' duration, the Fund may provide that the duration of a basic period shall be other than five years. Because of difficulties in projecting future reserve needs and the supply of reserves, it was proposed and agreed that the first basic period should be three years.

The actual amounts allocated on January 1 of each of the three years 1970–72 were SDR 3,414 million, SDR 2,949 million, and SDR 2,952 million, respectively, for a total of SDR 9,315 million. These amounts were calculated as a uniform percentage of each participant's quota in the Fund on the day before the allocation. The percentages were 16.8 percent, 10.7 percent, and 10.6 percent, respectively. (The percentages varied because of changes in quotas and in participation in the Special Drawing Account.)

Main Features of the SDR Facility

The principal characteristics of the SDR allocated on January 1, 1970 were as follows:

(1) Its value was equivalent to 0.886671 gram of fine gold, that is, SDR 1 = US$1.

(2) Its rate of interest was set at 1½ percent per annum. The Fund was empowered to raise this rate up to 2 percent or equal to the rate of remuneration paid on creditor positions in the General Account, whichever was higher, or lower it to 1 percent or the rate of remuneration, whichever was lower.

(3) Interest was payable by the Fund to each holder on the amount of its holdings of SDRs, and charges at the same rate as the interest rate were payable by each participant on the amount of its net cumulative allocation. Thus, if a participant in the course of a year had holdings on average above its allocations, it received net interest, and if its holdings on average were below its net cumulative allocation, it paid net charges. The total amount paid in interest equaled the amount of charges paid.

(4) Participants could use their holdings of SDRs in three principal ways: (a) to obtain foreign exchange from other participants designated (i.e., required) by the Fund to receive the SDRs being used; (b) by agreement with another participant to obtain balances of the user's own currency held by that participant; and (c) to settle obligations to repurchase balances of a participant's currency from or to pay charges to the Fund's General Account.

SDRs could not be used, however, to obtain foreign exchange through the designation mechanism or to obtain balances of the user's own currency in a bilateral transaction unless the user had a balance of payments need. In other words, a participant could not use its SDRs simply to change the composition of its reserves.

If so designated by the Fund, participants were obligated to provide their own currency to another participant and accept SDRs in return. Limitations were specified in the Articles.

Neither could a participant use all its SDRs over a period without being required to reconstitute a minimum proportion of its holdings. Two rules had to be observed: One was that a participant, over five-year periods, had to maintain an average SDR holding of not less than 30 percent of its average allocation. The second rule was a more general requirement that a participant pay "due regard to the desirability of pursuing over time a balanced relationship" between its holdings of SDRs and its holdings of other reserve assets.

As the unit of value of the SDR was equivalent to 0.888671 gram of fine gold and as all transfers of SDRs between participants were made in exchange for currency, it was necessary to transform the gold value of the SDR into a value in terms of the currency being used. The method employed was a simple one whereby the gold value of the SDR and the par value of the U.S. dollar were used to determine the SDR-U.S. dollar rate; the SDR exchange rates for other currencies were then calculated from their representative market exchange rates for the U.S. dollar. These representative rates were defined by decisions of the Fund after consultation with each member and were such that any participant using SDRs received the same value whatever currencies were provided by the participant to whom the SDRs were transferred and whichever participant provided those currencies.

Subsequently, the representative rates became the basis for valuing the Fund's holdings of all members' currencies. A member's currency is revalued whenever it is used by the Fund in a transaction with another member, and all currency holdings are revalued as of April 30 each year.

The SDR was the unit of account for recording all operations in the Special Drawing Account from January 1, 1970, and in March 1972, it was decided to express the Fund's own accounts in SDRs instead of U.S. dollars.

The initial characteristics of the SDR reflected an understandable caution in the deliberate creation of a new reserve asset and did not make it as attractive to its holders as some other reserve assets. This applied particularly to its interest rate and its usability.

In the first basic period 1970–72, allocations of SDRs totaled just over SDR 9.3 billion. Total gross transfers of SDRs in the same period amounted to about SDR 3.7 billion, or about 40 percent of the stock. Of this SDR 3.7 billion of turnover, about half consisted of transfers between participants, roughly divided in equal proportions between transactions with designation and bilateral transactions. The other half consisted of transactions between participants and the Fund's General Account through which all the Fund's operations and transactions were conducted, except those involving SDRs, which were conducted through the Special Drawing Account.

At the end of the first basic period, it was possible to make the following observations about the new reserve asset:

First, the design of the SDR facility had stood up well to its early tests. In particular, the designation mechanism had functioned satisfactorily and had assured participants with a balance of payments need that they could use SDRs to obtain foreign exchange needed to make foreign payments for goods or services. The SDR could also be freely used to make certain payments to the Fund, namely, in repurchases of members' currencies held by the Fund as a result of their use of the Fund's resources and the payment of charges for the use of the Fund's resources.

Second, there had been no rush by participants with a balance of payments need to divest themselves of SDRs—the turnover was relatively low—and it was soon apparent that many central banks were willing holders of the asset.

Third, as it became increasingly evident in later years, there was, nevertheless, a need to enhance the attractiveness of the SDR as a reserve asset.

By the end of 1973, it was generally felt that the SDR should become the principal reserve asset of the international monetary system, and this was expressly stated in the Outline of Reform presented in June 1974 by the Committee on Reform of the International Monetary System and Related Issues (Committee of Twenty).

Evolution of the SDR Since 1970

Prior to the Second Amendment of the Articles

The Outline of Reform represented two years of intensive preparatory work in a period of recurrent stress in the international monetary system, which saw the eventual breakdown of the Bretton Woods system. There were periodic, severe disturbances in the major exchange markets. In August 1971, the United States suspended convertibility of the U.S. dollar into gold for official holders. Subsequently, a number of major countries adopted floating exchange rates, which, however, were managed by the respective national authorities and not left free to move in accord with market forces. These developments, and two others described below, had important consequences for the SDR as regards its value, its method of valuation in terms of currencies, and its interest rates—that is, the effective yield of the SDR.

The other two developments were (1) the growing willingness of countries to hold their currency reserves in assets denominated in currencies other than the U.S. dollar—a process that came to be known as the multicurrency reserve system—and (2) a very large expansion in international liquidity. As noted earlier, in the period immediately prior to 1970, there had been great concern about the decline in the ratio of reserves to trade and a general expectation of a global need—in a world of fixed par values that were adjustable by individual Fund members only to correct a fundamental disequilibrium—to supplement international liquidity. Expectations, whether great or small, are not always realized, however, and in the event there was a sharp expansion in total official holdings of reserve assets comprising gold (valued at SDR 35 an ounce), SDRs, reserve positions in the Fund, and foreign exchange. These holdings almost doubled from about SDR 79 billion at the end of 1969 to over SDR 152 billion at the end of 1973. The SDR allocations were a relatively minor factor in this expansion, which occurred principally in foreign exchange holdings, particularly holdings of U.S. dollars. Deficits in the U.S. balance of payments on official settlements led to an increase over these years of almost SDR 50 billion in the official claims of other countries on the United States.

Two other factors also had major implications for the SDR: (1) the growth and closer integration of capital markets, which improved access by countries to international borrowing facilities, especially the Eurocurrency markets; and (2) the adoption of widespread managed floating of exchange rates by the major industrial countries. Consequently, there was no global need to supplement reserves, and no allocations of SDRs were made in the second basic period 1973–77.

When the SDR facility was being developed, another expectation was that, with its value guaranteed in terms of gold and with any currency revaluations in terms of gold likely to be relatively few on the basis of experience since 1946, the value of the SDR would at least be maintained in terms of currencies. This expectation had been an important factor in setting the SDR interest rate at 1½ percent. However, as early as 1972, it was recognized that a new approach to the value of the SDR would need to be introduced or an increase in its interest rate might be required.

With effect from July 1, 1974, major adaptations were made in the method of valuing the SDR and in determining its interest rate. Instead of the de facto link with the U.S. dollar, it was decided to value the SDR on the basis of a basket of the currencies of 16 countries that had a share in world trade of goods and services in excess of 1 percent on average over the five-year period 1968–72. This basket was later adjusted in July 1978 by the elimination of two currencies and the addition of two others. The interest rate was raised to 5 percent, subject to adjustment at six-month intervals according to a formula related to changes in the combined market interest rate calculated on the basis of domestic interest rates for short-term instruments in France, the Federal Republic of Germany, Japan, the United Kingdom, and the United States.

Although these changes improved the characteristics of the SDR, further steps were still needed to improve its usability. The implementation of such steps, however, had to await the Second Amendment of the Fund's Articles.

Since the Second Amendment of the Articles

On April 1, 1978, the Second Amendment of the Articles of Agreement entered into effect. With regard to the role of the SDR, the amended Articles expressly stated: "Each member undertakes to collaborate with the Fund and with other members in order to ensure that the policies of the member with respect to reserve assets shall be consistent with the objectives of promoting better international surveillance of international liquidity and making the special drawing right the principal reserve asset in the international monetary system." In addition, the amended Articles provided for radical changes in the role of gold aimed at reducing its importance in the international monetary system.

The developments and measures described below also indicate the present role of the SDR in international transactions:

The third basic period began on January 1, 1978, and based on a proposal by the Managing Director concurred in by the Executive Board, the Board of Governors resolved in December 1978 to make allocations of SDR 4 billion on January 1 of 1979, 1980, and 1981. The total of SDR allocations now amounts to SDR 21,433 million. All 146 members of the Fund are participants in the Special Drawing Rights Department, and all except 5, which joined the Fund after January 1, 1981, have received SDRs in allocations. The People's Republic of China received allocations totaling SDR 236.8 million and, on April 30, 1982, held SDR 215.7 million.

Another step, taken with effect from January 1, 1981, was a change in the SDR valuation basket from 16 currencies to 5—the U.S. dollar, the deutsche mark, the Japanese yen, the French franc, and the pound sterling—and its unification with the interest rate basket. The SDR interest rate, which from July 1, 1974 to June 30, 1976 averaged about 55 percent of the combined market rate determined by the interest rate basket, had been successively raised by Fund decisions to 60 percent and then to 80 percent of the combined market rate, and finally, with effect from May 1, 1981, it was raised to 100 percent. The actual SDR interest rate (and the SDR rate of charge) for the quarter that began on July 1, 1982 was 12.01 percent.

These changes meant that the SDR had finally been adapted to the prevailing international system of multiple reserve currencies and its yield had been adjusted to the market. In 1981, it thus became broadly competitive with similar holdings of the five major currencies. Its role as a reserve asset and a store of value was correspondingly enhanced.

The amended Articles and Fund decisions taken under their provisions represented other steps that helped to improve both the liquidity and usability of the SDR:

In the amended Articles, participants were allowed to use their SDRs to obtain currency in transactions by agreement with other participants (i.e., bilateral transactions), without regard to the requirement of need and without the necessity for specific authorization by the Fund.

The amended Articles also gave the Fund the authority to prescribe or permit operations in which participants may use SDRs by agreement without exchanging them directly for currency. In late 1978 and early 1979, the Fund adopted decisions that permit holders to use SDRs to settle financial obligations (other than to make donations), to make loans of SDRs at interest rates and maturities agreed between the parties, and to use SDRs in interest payments and repayment of principal. It was also decided to permit the use of SDRs as security for the discharge of financial obligations (again, other than to make donations).

The constraint of the reconstitution requirement was first eased by reducing the limit of 30 percent to 15 percent, with effect from January 1, 1979, and on April 30, 1980, it was removed altogether.

In late 1979 and early 1980, further decisions were taken to extend the usability of the SDR. Participants were allowed to use SDRs in swap arrangements and forward operations against currency or another monetary asset, other than gold, and to use them in donations.

Fund members are now required to pay all charges due to the General Resources Account in SDRs and may of course continue to make repurchases of the Fund's holdings of their currency in SDRs. Under the Seventh General Review of Quotas, participants were required to pay 25 percent of their increased quota subscriptions in SDRs, and new members may also be authorized to use SDRs in part payment of their quota subscriptions.

For some time before the Second Amendment of the Articles entered into effect, the Fund channeled back to members much of the inflow of SDRs to the Fund by transfers of SDRs to members making purchases from the General Resources Account. Many did so and converted all or part of the amounts of SDRs obtained in this way into foreign exchange through the designation mechanism.

SDRs have been used to denominate the amounts in recent borrowing agreements between the Fund and member governments, monetary authorities, and the Bank for International Settlements. Some of these agreements permit the lender to exchange a loan claim on the Fund for promissory notes in bearer form that would be transferable to other parties, official or private.

Prescribed holders of SDRs

Under the Articles, the Fund is authorized to prescribe as holders of SDRs nonmember countries, members that are nonparticipants in the Special Drawing Rights Department, institutions that perform functions of a central bank for more than one member, and other official entities. In October 1982, 13 institutions had prescribed holder status. Institutions that are prescribed by the Fund as holders of SDRs may engage in any of these operations, but they are not eligible to receive SDRs in allocations, to use the designation mechanism, or to deal in SDRs with the Fund's General Account, except if they are lenders to the Fund. In that case, they may, under the individual lending agreements, receive interest and principal repayments in SDRs.

Several of these institutions have engaged in transactions and operations in SDRs, and as a group they held SDRs amounting to almost SDR 4.3 million at the end of April 1982. Thus, a number of major institutions are in a legal position to acquire, hold, and use SDRs as they deem advisable under the relevant decisions of the Fund.

The SDR as a unit of account and currency peg

The SDR has been used as a unit of account in private market transactions, such as the acceptance of SDR-denominated deposits by banks and the issuance of bonds, syndicated bank loans, and certificates of deposit denominated in SDRs. An interesting although as yet very limited development is its use as a unit for invoicing private international transactions in goods and services. Some 15 international organizations use the SDR as their unit of account or as the basis of their accounting unit. The SDR is also used as a standard of value in a significant number of international conventions.

Sixteen member countries peg their exchange rates to the SDR. As at June 30, 1982, 23 Fund members, including the People's Republic of China, pegged their currencies to a composite other than the SDR.

The use of the SDR as a unit of account to denominate a wide range of financial instruments and obligations began in 1975 with a bond issue and was given considerable impetus in 1981 from the simplification of the SDR valuation basket. However, the market in SDR-denominated assets is a small segment of the total private market. What is of particular significance is whether the development of what may be conveniently termed the "private SDR" is conducive to enhancing the role of the SDR itself as a reserve asset. I find it difficult to imagine otherwise, because a complementary "private SDR" opens up possibilities, even though their realization may be some time in the future, of linking the "private SDR" in some way with the SDR as a means of helping in the development of a more stable international payments system.

The position of the SDR today

In total amount, SDRs constitute a relatively small proportion of officially held reserves, and it is uncertain whether the stock of SDRs will be increased in the near future. At the end of April 1982, total reserves excluding gold of all countries amounted to SDR 325 billion, of which SDRs accounted for just under 5 percent. On the other hand, all 146 Fund members are participants in the Special Drawing Rights Department, and a significant number of major international institutions are prescribed holders of SDRs.

Although participants and prescribed holders are able to use their SDRs freely in a wide variety of ways, in fact, the major uses by participants are to make certain payments to the Fund itself, to obtain foreign exchange through the designation mechanism, or to obtain SDRs needed to settle financial obligations to the Fund by engaging in bilateral transactions. In the last few years, the amount of bilateral transactions by agreement between participants has increased both in number and value. A growing number of participants have been willing to provide SDRs in such transactions, and the Fund staff has been able to informally bring together parties to bilateral transactions. Some of the prescribed holders have not as yet engaged in transactions and operations in SDRs. The use of SDRs in loans and in settlement of financial obligations is growing; however, there has been no use under the decisions that allow for wider use of SDRs as security for the discharge of financial obligations or in swaps, forward operations, and donations.

The characteristics of the SDR have been greatly improved over the years—its value is more stable in terms of currencies than any single currency, and its interest rate is the average of short-term rates in the five major centers. With its effective yield comparable to the yield on a multireserve currency holding, it is an attractive asset for a monetary authority or central bank to hold as part of its foreign reserves.

The SDR, however, is subject to the constraint that the designation mechanism requires participants judged by the Fund to be sufficiently strong to accept SDRs up to a point at which their holdings of SDRs in excess of net cumulative allocations are equal to twice their net cumulative allocations. Thus, there remains a degree of compulsion in the operation of the SDR facility, and participants do not completely control their holdings of the asset.

The use of the SDR as a unit of account outside the circle of official holders has been an encouraging development which, as it expands further, can be expected to contribute appreciably to the progress of the SDR as the principal reserve asset.

Prospects for the SDR

In examining the prospects for the SDR, it is important to keep a sense of time. In a historical perspective, its evolution has been over a very brief period, and although the recent pace of change has been rapid in some other areas, such as in international communications, I doubt whether it is either reasonable or realistic to expect a similar pace of change in the international monetary system. In analyzing the prospects for the SDR, it is also important to bear in mind that reaching international agreement on what changes in its characteristics are necessary and feasible to enhance its role in the system is not likely to be a quick process. Moreover, the international monetary system is not static, and it is advisable to guard against forming firm opinions about a future monetary system based on the current situation.

Some years ago, a phrase often used by a central banker in my own country, New Zealand, was "the inevitability of gradualness." If one subscribed to such an optimistic doctrine, one would argue with regard to the SDR that a gradual approach means that it would inevitably evolve as the principal reserve asset of the international monetary system. Nonsubscribers to this doctrine might argue quite differently. Some might state that the role of the SDR so far has been a relatively modest one, that its share in the total non-gold reserves of countries is no bigger now than when SDRs were first allocated, and that it is by no means certain that a gradual approach will result in its becoming the principal reserve asset. Others may take the view that, notwithstanding the difficulties in reaching international agreement, dramatic rather than gradual changes in the role and stature of the SDR in the international monetary system are not to be precluded.

Without subscribing to a doctrine of inevitability, I am nonetheless inclined to a pragmatic view that progress will be gradual. In this context, three questions need to be considered: Is there scope at present to improve the characteristics of the SDR? If there is, and it is utilized, would the role of the SDR be appreciably enhanced? If so, would further progress need to be made before it could be fairly claimed that the SDR is the principal reserve asset?

Under the present Articles, it would be possible to change some of the present characteristics of the SDR in a number of ways. The interest rate, for example, could be determined more frequently than once a quarter, and interest (and charges) could be paid more frequently than once a year. Such changes would make the SDR more comparable to reserve currencies as regards the calculation and payment of interest. The interest return could also be made more competitive with the return on other reserve assets. This could be achieved by setting the rate higher than 100 percent of the combined market rate or by revising the present interest rate basket to include instruments that carry higher interest rates. Such changes would bring the SDR interest rate better in line with market rates for the "private SDR," particularly those in the form of claims on private banks.

The liquidity and usability of the SDR may be improved, even if marginally, by simplifying the present reporting required by the Fund from participants and prescribed holders when they use or acquire SDRs and by developing a more active market in SDRs by extending the Fund's present activity in informally helping to bring together possible parties to a transaction or operation in SDRs. These and other ideas need more detailed consideration before specific proposals to implement them can be developed. The SDR is still not widely known by the public at large—it is not a tangible asset like currency and it lacks an easily understood symbol.

More fundamental issues, however, are involved in any effort to assess longer-run prospects for the SDR. Central among these issues is the manner in which international financial relations may be conducted in the future; the objectives that will be sought through international monetary cooperation and the role of the SDR in serving those objectives; the future supply of SDRs; and whether the SDR could and would be usable outside the present circle of official holders and the Fund, if not directly by the nonofficial sector, then indirectly by establishing a mechanism whereby national monetary authorities could exchange SDRs against private assets or liabilities denominated in terms of the SDR.

Judging by recent history, these issues most likely will not be settled either easily or quickly. In the meantime, however, it seems probable that further technical improvements will be made in the characteristics of the existing SDR; that the use of the SDR as a unit of account will continue to grow in both the official and private sectors, especially if different exchange rate relationships develop among the major currencies; and that, in the context of present international monetary arrangements, the SDR will continue to play a significant role in facilitating trade and financial transactions and in contributing to financial stability.

Hence, as regards the objective of making the SDR the principal reserve asset in the international monetary system, I would say that further progress will first be necessary in resolving the issues I have just mentioned before it could be unequivocably said that the objective has been attained. There are, however, reasons for optimism. For 36 years, the Fund has been an example of effective international collaboration. Its membership has increased by more than 30 since the beginning of 1970, and it has accumulated more experience in dealing with the problems of general instability and with the very difficult problems of individual member countries in establishing and maintaining a secure basis for economic growth. The private component of the international financial system is becoming more familiar with the SDR. While the amount of SDRs and members' official assets denominated in SDRs, such as reserve positions in the Fund, constitute a small proportion of international reserves, it is nonetheless a most significant one in demonstrating the willingness of Fund members to hold such assets. I think it is fair to say that there is more general awareness of the mutual interdependence and integration of national economies and of the need for stable domestic and international economic environments if development efforts are to proceed and yield results close to their objectives.

As a pragmatist, I conclude that considerable progress will need to be made to establish the SDR as the principal reserve asset in the international monetary system. I believe, however, that it will eventually be made.

Related Reading

Byrne, William J., "Evolution of the SDR, 1974–81," *Finance & Development,* International Monetary Fund and World Bank (Washington), Vol. 19 (September 1982), pp. 31–33.

Committee on Reform of the International Monetary System and Related Issues, *International Monetary Reform: Documents of the Committee of Twenty* (Washington, International Monetary Fund, 1974).

Cutler, David S., and Dhruba Gupta, "SDRs: Valuation and Interest Rate," *Finance & Development,* International Monetary Fund and World Bank (Washington), Vol. 11 (December 1974), pp. 18–21.

Gold, Joseph, *Special Drawing Rights: Character and Use,* IMF Pamphlet Series, No. 13, 2nd edition (Washington, 1970).

——————, *The Second Amendment of the Fund's Articles of Agreement,* IMF Pamphlet Series, No. 25 (Washington, 1978).

——————, *SDRs, Currencies, and Gold: Fifth Survey of New Legal Developments,* IMF Pamphlet Series, No. 36 (Washington, 1981).

Habermeier, Walter, *Operations and Transactions in SDRs: The First Basic Period,* IMF Pamphlet Series, No. 17 (Washington, 1973).

Hooke, A.W., *The International Monetary Fund: Its Evolution, Organization, and Activities,* IMF Pamphlet Series, No. 37, 2nd edition (Washington, 1982).

International Monetary Fund, *International Reserves: Needs and Availability* (Washington, 1970).

——————, *Reform of the International Monetary System: A Report by the Executive Directors to the Board of Governors* (Washington, 1972).

Polak, J.J., *Some Reflections on the Nature of Special Drawing Rights,* IMF Pamphlet Series, No. 16 (Washington, 1971).

——————, *Valuation and Rate of Interest of the SDR,* IMF Pamphlet Series, No. 18 (Washington, 1974).

——————, *Thoughts on an International Monetary Fund Based Fully on the SDR,* IMF Pamphlet Series, No. 28 (Washington, 1979).

Summary of Discussion

Much of the discussion on the SDR was of a technical nature, concerning such matters as the uses of the SDR, the countries that could receive allocations of SDRs, the institutions that could hold SDRs, and the formulas that were used to determine the value of and the rate of interest on the SDR. However, attention was also paid to more policy-oriented matters, including the roles assigned to the SDR under the First and Second Amendments of the Fund's Articles of Agreement, the steps that could be taken to enhance the role of the SDR as the principal reserve asset of the international monetary system, and the reasons why no allocations of SDRs had been made or provided for since the end of the third basic period in 1981.

The First Amendment specified a rather modest role for the SDR— it was to supplement existing reserve assets, which were to remain the major components of international reserves. The Second Amendment, however, called for the SDR to become the principal reserve asset of the international monetary system, implying that SDRs should at some time replace at least part of the gold and foreign exchange holdings in international reserves. It was suggested by some participants that this indicated an inconsistency between the two Amendments and that developments since the Second Amendment came into effect indicated that the supplementary role of the SDR was still predominant.

The Fund staff argued that the difference between the roles described in the two Amendments reflected not an inconsistency but an evolution of thinking about the SDR. The objective expressed in the First Amendment— of being a supplementary reserve asset— was about the most that could reasonably be expected at that time of the new and untested asset. By the time the Second Amendment was being drafted, however, the SDR, despite its early limitations, was becoming increasingly accepted, and confidence was growing that it could eventually become the principal reserve asset of the international monetary system. The Fund staff also noted that, while the transition from supplementary to principal reserve asset had certainly not been made, the capacity of the SDR to fill the latter role had increased considerably since the Second Amendment entered into effect. The method of valuing the SDR had been simplified, the rate of interest on the SDR had been raised to the market level, and the range of uses to which the SDR could be put had been widened. As a result of these improvements, particularly the rise in the interest rate, it had become possible to abolish the requirement that members hold minimum average balances of SDRs.

Participants observed that there were important advantages to having the SDR as the principal reserve asset of the system. These included the distribution among all Fund members—and not just among those whose currencies were used as reserve assets—of the seignorage involved in reserve creation and the possibility of more effective control over international liquidity. This led to a discussion of the actions that could be taken, by the Fund and others, to promote the SDR. It was suggested that the Fund could further improve the characteristics of the asset, although it was recognized that scope was now limited for additional progress in this direction. The Fund could also set an example by making more use of SDRs and less use of currencies in its financial transactions with members. The most important action, however, would be for private economic agents to denominate their international transactions in SDRs. If banks were to open accounts denominated in SDRs, if depositors were to use these accounts, and if firms were to denominate their external borrowings in SDRs, the SDR would be well-placed to become the principal reserve asset of the international monetary system.

Participants expressed considerable interest in the reasons why the Fund had not allocated any SDRs in 1982 and had not decided to make any allocations in 1983. The Fund staff pointed out that a decision to allocate SDRs required the support of 85 percent of the Fund's voting power. The necessary support had not been forthcoming for allocations in 1982 or 1983, largely because of concern among some of the major industrial countries that an allocation might raise doubts as to the resolve of the authorities in these countries to eliminate inflation. They added that the Managing Director was keeping in close contact with Executive Directors on the issue and would make a proposal for a resumption of allocations when a consensus in favor of such action emerged.

The Role of the Fund
in Developing Countries

A.W. Hooke

The International Monetary Fund is not directly responsible for the promotion of economic development. Its founding fathers made a clear distinction between the goals of balance of payments adjustment and economic development and argued that it was important to have separate institutions for pursuing these goals. They maintained that this separation would facilitate progress toward attainment of the Fund's goals and would reduce the risks of both excessive centralization of power and costly errors of judgment. Thus, the Bretton Woods Conference of July 1944, at which the original Articles of Agreement of the Fund were drafted, also provided for the creation of a second institution, the International Bank for Reconstruction and Development (World Bank), which would tackle problems of economic development.

The drafters of the Fund's Articles were, however, convinced that successful performance by the Fund would facilitate the economic development of its members. Article I includes, as a purpose of the Fund, promotion of the expansion and balanced growth of international trade. The Article indicates that this will contribute to the maintenance of high levels of employment and real income and to the development of the productive resources of all members.

The Fund's original Articles of Agreement did not distinguish between developing and developed countries They did not, unlike those of the General Agreement on Tariffs and Trade and the International Development Association (IDA), prescribe rights and duties that differ according to the member's stage of economic development. Subject now to a few express exceptions, the principle of uniformity remains implicit in the Articles and has been carried over into the policies adopted by the Fund's governing bodies.

Nevertheless, the Fund has adopted certain policies that, while preserving this formal equality, do have the indirect effect of focusing on certain identifiable groups of countries. Several of the Fund's financial facilities are directed toward problems that are especially acute among developing countries, whereas none is focused on the special requirements of industrial countries. Similarly, the Fund's technical assistance and training activities are geared primarily to the needs of developing countries.

The first part of this paper discusses the present role of the Fund in relation to the developing countries. It pays only limited attention to the benefits that these countries share on a roughly even basis with the industrial countries, since these benefits have already been covered in earlier papers. Instead, it places emphasis on the special benefits that accrue to or the special costs that are incurred by developing countries. The second part of the paper considers some of the proposals that have been made to increase the usefulness of the Fund to the developing countries. The proposals discussed are designed to increase the flow of financial resources to developing countries and to make these resources available on easier terms.

The Present Situation

The role of the Fund can be evaluated by examining the contribution the Fund makes in carrying out each of its major functions. For this purpose, it is useful to distinguish four functions: (1) the supervision of exchange rate policies and exchange practices; (2) the provision of financial resources in support of programs of balance of payments adjustment; (3) the regulation of international liquidity; and (4) the provision of advice on matters related to the first three functions.

The supervisory function

Members have a general obligation to collaborate with the Fund and with each other to promote orderly exchange arrangements and a stable system of exchange rates. They also have some more specific obligations, intended to further the same objectives. The Fund oversees the compliance of members with these obligations. It has formulated a set of principles to guide members' exchange rate policies and exercises firm surveillance over these policies.

Developing countries can benefit, along with other countries, from the Fund's exercise of surveillance. By promoting the convergence of economic policies and conditions in member countries, especially in the major trading countries, surveillance contributes to a more stable pattern of exchange rates. The benefits from this include a more appropriate level and composition of output in the tradables sector, as a result of the positive contribution that more predictable exchange rates make to sound investment and production decisions in that sector. They also include greater ease of debt management, and of reserves management, because of smaller movements in exchange rates between currencies in which exports and debts are denominated in the first case and imports and reserves are denominated in the second.

It has been argued that surveillance over exchange rate policies can be exercised more effectively over countries that seek access to Fund resources than over other countries and that it therefore tends to bear more heavily on the former group of countries. Since, in recent years, only developing countries have sought to use Fund resources, surveillance, it is claimed, has operated unfairly against the developing countries.

There may be some truth in this argument. Since 1978, only developing countries have borrowed from the Fund. The Fund has, naturally, made such access conditional on these countries' adopting appropriate policies of balance of payments adjustment. Its ability to influence the policies of countries that have not approached the Fund for assistance has been more limited.

It is useful, however, to remember that, even if all the countries that are not using the Fund's resources were to adopt the adjustment policies deemed appropriate for them by the international community, there would still be a need for stronger adjustment measures by many countries that are borrowing from the Fund, especially those where excessively expansionary policies have contributed to their external difficulties.

The second aspect of the Fund's supervisory role concerns exchange practices. The Fund tries to promote a system for current account payments in which individuals and enterprises can freely exchange domestic currency for any foreign currency, in order to pay for imports or transfers, at rates of exchange that do not depend on the types of imports or transfers. Thus, members of the Fund are expected, among other things, to avoid restrictions on current payments and transfers, multiple currency practices, and discriminatory currency arrangements, unless they receive temporary authority from the Fund to do otherwise. The Fund supervises members' compliance with these requirements.

In general, members of the Fund benefit from the mutual observance of the code on exchange practices. It permits firms producing exportables to sell in the most profitable markets and firms trading in importables to buy in the cheapest markets. Compared with the system of exchange practices of, say, the 1930s, this produces a better international division of labor; within countries, it results in a much more efficient allocation of resources between the tradables and nontradables sectors as well as within the tradables sector, and thus in a higher level of real income.

During the early years of the Fund's operations, the great majority of developing countries maintained extensive restrictions on current account payments. However, as the world first recovered from the dislocations of the war and then moved through a period of unprecedented prosperity in the late 1950s and 1960s, an increasing number dismantled these restrictions. By the early 1970s, many developing countries had adopted the Fund's code on exchange practices, and a large part of the remainder had reduced considerably the coverage and severity of their restrictions.

The situation has changed to a large extent in recent years, with the spread of restrictions on the use of foreign currencies to service external debts. This development has been confined mainly to the non-oil developing countries. As a result partly of deterioration in their terms of trade from about the mid-1970s, slower growth in the industrial countries, and higher interest rates, these countries have been faced with sharply rising debt servicing commitments, and a growing number have been unable to meet them. The number of countries with payments arrears rose from 15 in 1975 to 32 in 1981.

Members of the Fund are expected to obtain approval for restrictions on the use of foreign currency to service external debts. The Fund normally makes such approval conditional on the member's formulating an adjustment program that is likely to be effective in bringing the member's balance of payments to a stage where it can remove the restriction. Agreement with the Fund on a program is frequently helpful in debt renegotiations and in promoting renewed capital inflows.

The financial function

On behalf of its members, the Fund administers a pool of financial resources. These resources comprise the currencies of members, special drawing rights (SDRs), and gold. They are derived from quota subscriptions, net earnings by the Fund, and borrowings. The Fund uses them to provide financial assistance to members experiencing balance of payments difficulties, to enable these members either to finance their deficit, if this is deemed to be the appropriate response, or to eliminate or offset its causes through policies that are not detrimental to the prosperity of the member or the international community.

The Fund's oldest lending policy, the credit tranche policy, is not designed to discriminate in favor of any particular group of member countries. Under this policy, the Fund makes financial resources available to members experiencing balance of payments difficulties of a general nature. Developing countries benefit both directly and indirectly from the policy. They benefit directly when they experience balance of payments difficulties and are enabled, by having access to resources under this policy, to seek a smoother and less costly path of balance of payments adjustment. They benefit indirectly when the policy is used by other countries, and they are protected from the consequences of unduly abrupt adjustment in these countries.

The Fund's three other permanent lending facilities—the compensatory financing, buffer stock financing, and extended Fund facilities—while formally accessible to all members, have provided assistance mainly to developing countries. They do this by addressing balance of payments problems that could be experienced by any country but, in fact, are most prevalent and acute among the developing countries. The compensatory financing facility was introduced in 1963 to enable the Fund to provide assistance to exporters of primary products and was thus expected to be of special benefit to developing countries. Its coverage was widened in 1981 to include compensation for excesses in the costs of cereal imports, partly in response to a suggestion by the Food and Agriculture Organization and the World Food Council that the Fund consider extending such assistance to its low-income members. When the buffer stock financing facility was introduced, the Fund announced that it was intended essentially for "members in their capacity as exporters of primary products." The Fund recognized the right of importing countries that contribute to buffer stock arrangements also to draw under the facility, but anticipated that such contributions could rarely be expected to have a significant effect on the balance of payments of these countries and that their need to draw would therefore be minimal. The extended Fund facility is aimed at countries with balance of payments problems that are attributable to structural weaknesses of a kind that are most common in developing countries, or whose balance of payments situation is too weak to permit them to mount an effective development program. While, in principle, this latter situation could obtain in an industrial country, in practice, it is limited to the poorest developing countries.

The four temporary financial facilities that have been established by the Fund—the 1974 and 1975 oil facilities, the supplementary financing facility, and the enlarged access policy—have also been of considerable benefit to the developing countries. Under the oil facilities, the Fund provided assistance to 55 member countries, 45 of which were developing countries. Both the supplementary financing facility and its successor, the enlarged access policy, have been used only by developing countries.

In fact, from the mid-1970s, most of the Fund's loan commitments and disbursements have been to developing countries. During 1974–81, it made commitments (net of cancellations) under stand-by and extended arrangements, the supplementary financing facility, and the enlarged access policy of SDR 32 billion; of this, all but SDR 6 billion was to developing countries. The Fund also made disbursements of SDR 13 billion under its other facilities during 1974–81, of which SDR 9 billion, or more than two thirds, was to developing countries. Disbursements under these facilities during 1979–81, of SDR 3.2 billion, were wholly to developing countries.

A less favorable development from the viewpoint of developing countries has been the shift from concessional to more commercial terms, for at least a portion of the finance. It was originally envisaged that members would use Fund resources for only short periods and that over time use would be spread fairly evenly among the entire membership. In line with this concept of mutual assistance, subscriptions were provided to the Fund free of cost, and the Fund was able to make them available on concessional terms to borrowing countries. However, at a fairly early stage, remuneration became payable to members whose currency subscriptions were used by the Fund. With capital subscriptions not keeping pace with the demand for Fund resources, the Fund has had to borrow at market-related interest rates, and this, together with increases in the rate of remuneration, has necessitated raising the charges it levies on its loans. Nevertheless, average charges are still well below market interest rates.

While the Fund does not formally discriminate among its members in making its own financial resources available to them, it does, through its administered accounts—such as the oil facility subsidy account and the supplementary financing facility subsidy account— provide some resources exclusively to developing countries. It can do this because, although these accounts have been set up by decisions of the Fund's Executive Board, their resources are separate from those of the Fund. Until recently, the Fund administered a Trust Fund that also provided assistance only to developing countries.

The Trust Fund, which was set up in 1976 and terminated in 1981, channeled profits from the sale of a portion of the Fund's gold to developing countries. It received profits of US$4.6 billion, distributed more than one fourth of this sum directly to 104 developing countries, and, after meeting expenses, loaned the remainder to eligible developing countries. The loans are highly concessional—they are for ten years, have a grace period of five years, and bear interest at the rate of 0.5 percent per annum. They are being repaid into the Fund's Special Disbursement Account.

The oil facility subsidy account assists eligible developing countries by subsidizing their interest payments on drawings made under the 1975 oil facility. The rate of subsidy has been 5 percentage points, reducing the effective cost to these countries of borrowing under the facility to about 2.7 percent per annum. The total subsidy paid through 1981 was SDR 50 million. The account will probably be terminated in 1983, when all drawings made under the 1975 oil facility will have been repaid.

The supplementary financing facility subsidy account reduces the cost to developing countries of borrowings made under the supplementary financing facility. It pays a subsidy of up to 3 percent of outstanding borrowings by 69 countries whose per capita incomes in 1979 did not exceed the level used to determine eligibility for access to funds from IDA. It also pays a subsidy of half that amount to a group of 14 higher-income developing countries.

The liquidity function

The supervisory and financial functions of the Fund were assigned to it in the original Articles of Agreement. Under the First Amendment of the Articles in July 1969, the Fund acquired an added function; henceforth, it was to regulate the supply of international liquidity so as to facilitate, among other things, avoidance in the world economy of stagnation and unemployment, on the one hand, and excess demand and inflation, on the other. To enable it to carry out this function, the Fund was given the authority to allocate (or cancel if necessary) agreed amounts of a new reserve asset, the SDR. Since then, the Fund has made allocations totaling SDR 21.4 billion, equivalent to a little under 4 percent of international reserve assets at the end of 1981, to participants in its Special Drawing Rights Department.

Appropriate allocations of SDRs contribute to the stable growth of the world economy, which is beneficial to both developing and industrial countries.

In addition, most developing countries receive a special financial benefit from allocations of SDRs. Participants in the Special Drawing Rights Department (currently, all Fund members) pay interest to the Fund on their cumulative allocations of SDRs. The rate of interest is the weighted average of interest rates on short-term domestic securities in the United States, the United Kingdom, the Federal Republic of Germany, France, and Japan. These are blue-chip securities, and the interest rate on them is well below the cost at which most developing countries can borrow in the international capital markets. By using SDRs allocated by the Fund in place of commercial borrowings to maintain reserves, developing countries benefit from this interest differential. The benefit is, of course, larger for the less creditworthy countries, and largest of all for the least creditworthy countries for which the availability rather than the cost of reserve assets is often the most important consideration.

The advisory function

Balance of payments difficulties may be caused by such factors as unexpected changes in the domestic or external environment or the adoption of overly ambitious economic and financial policies. However, they may also be caused by technical weaknesses in monetary, fiscal, and trade systems, by shortages of personnel skilled in the formulation and execution of policy, and by lack of reliable data on which to base policy decisions. Many countries, especially developing countries, have sought the assistance of the Fund in their efforts to overcome these latter difficulties. Since the Fund has built up considerable expertise in such areas and is able to tap additional expertise in member countries, it is well-placed to meet their requests. Such services are provided through technical assistance missions, field assignments, and studies and recommendations prepared at headquarters as well as through seminars and courses provided at headquarters and in member countries. The Fund also provides considerable technical assistance in the course of its regular consultation missions.

Technical assistance provided in the area of money and banking during the early years of the Fund was concerned mainly with the creation of new national currencies and of institutions to issue and regulate these. However, most members now have established currencies and central banks, and emphasis has switched to modernizing existing institutions and increasing the effectiveness of monetary policies. Assistance is provided by the staff of the Central Banking Department, who carry out research at and give advice from headquarters and undertake short missions to countries requesting assistance. However, most of the assistance is provided by a panel of outside experts, mainly staff from older central banks, universities, and the private sectors of member countries. About half of these outside experts now come from developing countries and are familiar with the environments and problems faced by the particular countries to which they are assigned. While the Fund selects and appoints the experts and pays their salaries, the experts work solely under the direction of their host institutions.

The Fund's involvement in providing technical assistance on fiscal matters reflects the importance of this sector in coping with balance of payments difficulties. Frequently, fiscal systems are not sufficiently developed for governments to be able to determine expenditure priorities, to provide adequate resources to finance planned expenditures, and to ensure that their budgets are executed reasonably in line with forecasts. To help overcome these difficulties, the Fund's Fiscal Affairs Department provides technical assistance on tax structures, introduction of new taxes, tax assessment and collection procedures, and investment incentive codes. It also provides assistance on budget preparation, expenditure control, government accounting systems, and other fiscal matters. A considerable amount of the assistance involves work in the field. For this purpose, the department makes its own staff available, especially for short-term projects. It also assigns outside experts, selected from a panel, generally for longer-term projects. These outside experts, unlike those assigned by the Central Banking Department, are solely responsible to and work under the direction of the Fiscal Affairs Department.

Most of the Fund's technical assistance in statistics is provided under the Central Bank Bulletin project. This project aims at establishing or improving central bank bulletins in member countries by providing these countries with advice on the nature and generation of data for the bulletins. The data set comprises the national accounts, production, prices, money and banking, government finance, external trade, the balance of payments, and other series that facilitate analysis of the balance of payments situation and prospects and matters affecting them. The Bureau of Statistics is responsible for the project.

The Fund's training program is similar to the technical assistance program and is directed mainly toward meeting the needs of developing country members. The program is organized and administered by the IMF Institute and includes courses on financial analysis and policy, balance of payments methodology, public finance, and government finance statistics. Participants are officials of member countries, mostly from finance ministries and central banks. Most of the courses are given in Washington, but the Institute has recently formed a separate division that sends staff on short-term teaching assignments to the larger developing countries or to new member countries.

Some Developing Country Proposals for Change

Many proposals have been made for changes in the Fund's policies and practices so as to make the organization more effective in meeting the special needs of developing countries. This part of the paper outlines some of these proposals and presents some of the arguments that have been put forward in favor of and against their adoption. The proposals concern limits on the Fund's financial assistance, the availability of a medium-term financial facility, conditionality, the Fund's gold holdings, and SDR allocations. In terms of the classification of functions used in the first part of this paper, the proposals are intended to increase the usefulness to developing countries of the Fund's financial and liquidity functions.

Limits on financial assistance

The maximum financial assistance that a member in balance of payments difficulties can obtain from the Fund under the latter's various financial facilities is tied to the member's quota in the Fund. Recent proposals for increasing potential access relative to quota have been based partly on the increase in current account deficits relative to world trade and the decrease in quotas relative to world trade that have occurred during the last decade as well as the growing difficulties many developing countries are experiencing in borrowing in international capital markets.

To a large extent, certain changes in Fund policies have already offset the relative increase in current account deficits and relative decline in quotas. Until the mid-1960s, the maximum assistance that a member could obtain from the Fund was normally limited to an amount equal to 100 percent of quota. Under the enlarged access policy, a member can now draw up to 150 percent of quota a year over a three-year period, with a ceiling on cumulative access, net of scheduled repurchases, of 600 percent of quota. In addition, a member can have drawings up to 125 percent of quota under the compensatory financing facility and 50 percent of quota under the buffer stock financing facility.

It has been argued that further easing of access would unduly mitigate against balance of payments adjustment. Indeed, it has been suggested that the Fund is already lending too much to deficit countries and that, rather than increasing its financing, it should be seeking to reduce the amounts it makes available. It has also been proposed that, as quotas are increased, access to resources relative to quotas should be reduced.

Establishment of a medium-term lending facility

The proposal that the Fund introduce a medium-term lending facility, with both disbursements and repayments spread over longer periods, is based partly on the greater importance of structural causes of balance of payments deficits as well as the sharp increase in the size of these deficits since the early 1970s. Measures to correct structural weaknesses are essentially supply-oriented and take a longer time to be effective than do demand-oriented measures. Because of this, and also because of the larger size of present deficits, members implementing programs of structural adjustment need a longer time to generate the external resources needed to complete repayments to the Fund.

It could be argued that the Fund already provides medium-term balance of payments assistance. Under the extended Fund facility, assistance is provided over a three-year period and repayments need not be completed for ten years. Resources may also be made available over a three-year period under a stand-by arrangement, but in this case they must be fully repaid within five years. The possibility of back-to-back arrangements offers scope for extending both the program and the repayment periods under stand-by as well as extended arrangements.

It has also been argued that creation of a longer-term facility runs the danger both of encouraging delays in adjustment and of moving the Fund outside its traditional area of competence into the field of development finance. For many situations, adjustment is more certain and less costly in terms of other goals when it is undertaken early and with a program designed to be implemented quickly rather than with measures spread over a protracted period. Also, some problems that have important implications for the balance of payments and can only be solved over a long period are essentially development problems. They call for assistance from bilateral aid donors and from international institutions such as the World Bank and regional development organizations, not for balance of payments assistance from the Fund.

Conditionality

Developing countries generally accept the need for the Fund to attach policy conditions to the use of its resources but have frequently expressed reservations about the nature and severity of this conditionality. Among their criticisms are the charges that the Fund's approach is excessively monetarist, that it does not make allowance for the causes of payments difficulties, and that the Fund's policy prescriptions impose a heavy burden on the poorest sections of the population.

The criticism that the Fund places excessive emphasis on monetary variables in assigning causes to balance of payments problems and in devising solutions to these problems is frequently associated with the argument that the Fund recommends policies that are unduly deflationary. Programs that are supported by the Fund under upper credit tranche or extended arrangements normally do include, as performance criteria, limits on the expansion of credit, the purpose of which is to contain the growth of aggregate demand. It can be argued that this is not inappropriate, since in many instances excess demand is an important factor contributing to the balance of payments difficulties that countries using the Fund's resources are trying to overcome. Even when this is not so, it may still be important to ensure that excess demand does not emerge and undermine the member's adjustment program. In this context, it is worth noting that the Fund's guidelines on conditionality include the prescription that performance clauses be no stronger than is necessary to ensure the success of the member's program.

Many agree with the view that the degree of conditionality should be lower when the causes of payments difficulties are beyond the control of the national authorities than when they can be attributed to inappropriate policies. However, balance of payments problems have to be solved whether their causes are within or beyond the control of the authorities. It can be argued that, for the purpose of formulating effective adjustment programs, the important causal distinction is between self-reversing and permanent factors. In the former, only minor changes or no policy changes at all may be required, even though the causes may reflect domestic policy actions. However, in the latter, quite strong measures might be called for, and a higher degree of conditionality could be appropriate, even if the causes are of external origin.

The argument that the Fund's prescriptions impose a heavy burden on the poorest sections of the population is based to some extent on what has actually happened in some cases where countries have introduced programs of balance of payments adjustment. Unfortunately, adjustment often imposes short-term costs on the poor, as well as on other segments of the population. However, the argument that the Fund is responsible seems to imply that it is the Fund, rather than the borrowing country's economic situation, that produces the need for adjustment. It also seems to imply that, when adjustment requires some reduction in domestic absorption, it is the Fund—and not the national authorities—that selects the measures that determine the distribution of this reduction. Supporters of the Fund's approach to conditionality (including representatives of many of the countries that supply it with usable resources) argue that members with serious balance of payments problems do not adopt adjustment programs just because the Fund believes they should do so; rather, the authorities of these countries choose to do so to avoid the consequences of continued imbalance that would eventually include exhaustion of their international reserves and borrowing power. By providing these countries with additional resources during the adjustment period, the Fund contributes to the solution, not to the cause, of their payments problems.

With respect to the second assumption, the Fund's guidelines on conditionality require that its performance criteria be restricted, as far as possible, to macroeconomic variables. The Fund must also be satisfied that the planned measures will be adequate to achieve the goals of members' programs, but it is not responsible for the selection of these measures. The national authorities must make the difficult choices that determine the manner in which any reduction in absorption is distributed among the different sections of their populations.

Gold holdings

The Fund holds about 104 million ounces of gold. At mid-1982 prices, the value of this gold exceeds that of the Fund's holdings of usable currencies. It has been recommended that the Fund use its gold to obtain additional resources by offering part of it as collateral against borrowings and by selling the remainder. The Fund could use the borrowings to increase lending and the sales receipts to increase subsidies (through administered accounts) to developing countries. Such use of the gold, it is claimed, would also further its demonetization and therefore strengthen the reserve asset role of the SDR.

The Articles specify various ways in which the Fund can use its gold holdings. Decisions on such use are, however, subject to high majorities and must, accordingly, reflect a broad consensus among the Fund's membership.

Opponents of the use of gold as collateral for borrowings argue that borrowed resources are less satisfactory than additional subscriptions, which are costless to the Fund, as a way of increasing resources. They also argue that, in a second-best context in which agreement on adequate quota increases cannot be obtained, the Fund should use its gold holdings to maintain a strong overall financial position rather than make them available as collateral for specific borrowings. This latter issue is, of course, essentially an empirical one, whose resolution depends on the perceptions of those from whom the Fund may need to borrow.

With respect to sales of gold by the Fund, opponents concede that these, like quota increases, could provide a costless increase in the Fund's loanable resources. However, they note that gold sales represent a change in the composition, not an increase in the level, of the Fund's total assets and that sales to finance subsidies would accordingly reduce the Fund's assets. Opponents of such tied sales argue that subsidies should be financed in a way that does not reduce the Fund's assets, such as by donations from members or—as is now being done for the supplementary financing facility subsidy account—from repayments of Trust Fund loans.

SDR-aid link

The Fund's Articles specify that allocations of SDRs be proportional to Fund quotas. This provision is based on the view that allocations should be neutral with respect to the liquidity needs of participants and that the best working guide to the pattern of liquidity needs is the distribution of Fund quotas.

Proposals to allocate a larger share of SDRs to developing countries were considered prior to the First Amendment of the Fund's Articles, and more extensively by the Committee on Reform of the International Monetary System and Related Issues (Committee of Twenty) during the deliberations leading up to the Second Amendment. The subject has been discussed in a number of different forums since then. These discussions have focused on the effects of a link on the volume of aid, on balance of payments adjustment, on inflation, and on the acceptability of the SDR as a reserve asset.

The most frequently used argument in favor of the link is that it would contribute to a more equitable distribution of world income by increasing the volume of aid. This was a stronger argument prior to May 1981, when the rate of interest on the SDR was below the market rate of interest and there would have been a large grant element in the transfer of SDRs to developing countries. Nevertheless, developing countries would still receive an immediate benefit from such transfers because, as noted earlier, many have to pay a premium to acquire reserve assets in the international capital markets. Critics of the link caution against overestimating the magnitude of the effect on aid. They argue that donor countries might respond to its adoption by reducing other forms of aid.

The Independent Commission on International Development Issues (Brandt Commission) emphasized the contribution that the link could make to the balance of payments adjustment process. The Commission argued that it was in the international interest for countries to be provided with sufficient short-term resources to permit them to avoid measures that could be harmful to their own economies or to those of other countries. It maintained that new reserve assets should therefore be allocated to countries that are most likely to incur balance of payments deficits, face high domestic costs of adjustment, and are least likely to be able to find alternative sources of finance. The Commission claimed that many developing countries are in this category. Against this view, it has been argued that a link arrangement that provided unconditional resources to the developing countries might ease their adjustment problems only so long as the additional resources were not anticipated; once these countries included the link-related SDRs in their forecasts, they could plan for and incur correspondingly larger payments deficits. Opponents of the link also question whether it is appropriate to reward countries for getting into balance of payments difficulties and point out that the incentives provided by such an approach could aggravate imbalances. They argue that, if additional resources are required to enable deficit countries to adjust their balance of payments while avoiding recourse to restrictive measures, the need is for more conditional resources under the Fund's lending facilities, not more unconditional resources in the form of SDR allocations.

A frequent objection to the link is that it might contribute to worldwide inflation, because it would give developing countries a greater incentive to seek large allocations and also because these countries have a higher propensity to use such allocations to pay for imports. On the first point, proponents of the link agree that the size of SDR allocations should be determined by the world's need for additional liquidity. Nevertheless, the criteria for determining the world's liquidity needs are not very precise, and acceptance of this principle cannot be expected to produce agreement on the appropriate size of allocations. A more effective safeguard against excessive allocations is the provision in the Articles of Agreement that decisions to allocate SDRs require an 85 percent majority of the Fund's voting power; this clearly precludes the developing countries' pushing through an allocation over the opposition of the industrial countries or even of the United States by itself or a small group of other major industrial countries. On the second point, it is generally conceded that introduction of the link would result in an effective transfer of newly created SDRs from countries wanting SDRs largely in order to hold them to countries seeking SDRs mostly in order to spend them. Developing countries respond to this argument by pointing out that the resulting higher propensity to spend out of total SDR allocations could be offset by a corresponding reduction in the size of the allocations.

Opponents of the link also claim that attempting to promote a development as well as a liquidity objective through the allocation of SDRs would unduly detract from the purely monetary role of the SDR and thereby reduce its acceptability as a reserve asset. However, supporters point out that, technically at least, there is nothing very complex about using two instruments—in this instance, the size and the pattern of the SDR allocation—to achieve two objectives. They also maintain that the acceptability of the SDR, an asset which has no counterpart liability, depends on the confidence of the larger and financially stronger countries (which tend to be net recipients of SDRs) that those with an obligation to pay interest charges on SDR allocations will continue to meet this obligation. They argue that developing countries will not have any financial incentive to default on their obligation if the present value of their future interest commitments on past allocations is less than their forecast of the present value of the grant element in future SDR allocations. They also note that the grant element in allocations is generally higher for developing countries than they are for industrial countries because of their lower credit rating and that these countries, therefore, have a greater interest in ensuring the continuation of allocations. Supporters of the link add that, in any case, the direction of the financial incentive is independent of the link—only the strength of the incentive is affected, this being tied to the sizes of their past and expected future allocations. Finally, they point out that default on the obligation to service SDRs would have major implications for a wide range of economic and financial relations and that the developing countries would not want to experience the effects of such a shock to the international monetary system.

Related Reading

Bird, Graham, "Developing Country Interests in Proposals for International Monetary Reform," in *Adjustment and Financing in the Developing World: The Role of the International Monetary Fund*, ed. by Tony Killick (Washington, 1982), pp. 198–232.

Gold, Joseph, "Professor Verwey, the International Monetary Fund, and Developing Countries," *The Indian Journal of International Law* (New Delhi), Vol. 21 (October–December 1981), pp. 497–512.

Hooke, A.W., "The Brandt Commission and International Monetary Issues," *Finance & Development*, International Monetary Fund and World Bank (Washington), Vol. 18 (June 1981), pp. 22–24.

Independent Commission on International Development Issues ("Brandt Commission"), *North-South: A Programme for Survival* (Cambridge, Massachusetts, 1980).

Summary of Discussion

Participants commended the Fund on the role it had played in providing developing countries with financial assistance to cope with their balance of payments difficulties. Some believed, however, that the Fund should increase the amounts of conditional and unconditional assistance it made available, especially to low-income developing countries. Some also expressed concern about the way in which the Fund exercised surveillance over its members and questioned whether its treatment was as evenhanded as the principle of uniformity of treatment required.

In the *World Economic Outlook* report of April 1982, the Fund staff projected a current account deficit for the non-oil developing countries in 1982 of almost US$100 billion, or about the same as the actual deficit registered in 1981. The *Outlook* also indicated rather bleak medium-term prospects for the non-oil developing countries—under one of its scenarios, the ratio of their current account deficit to exports of goods and services would be as high in 1986 as in 1982. In view of this, it was suggested, the Fund should give priority in its lending activities to the non-oil developing countries.

The Fund staff agreed with this view. They noted that, while the Fund was required to meet the needs of all its members in an equitable manner, these needs varied from time to time, and in recent years the countries with the greatest needs had been the non-oil developing countries. Not only were their current account deficits large, but also most did not have the easy access to international capital markets enjoyed by the industrial countries. As a result, virtually all of the Fund's lending during the last four years had been to the non-oil developing countries.

The amount that countries could draw from the Fund relative to quota had increased during the two preceding decades, from 100 percent for all drawings to 600 percent exclusive of drawings under the Fund's "low-conditionality" facilities. It was pointed out, however, that quotas had declined sharply relative to world trade and even more steeply relative to current account deficits. In view of this, it was argued, there should be a further substantial increase in the ratio of maximum potential access to quota, especially for the low-income developing countries. This could be done either by increasing the present ratio for "high-conditionality" finance or by creating a new facility that would not be affected by this ratio.

The Fund staff pointed out that a policy that would formally provide preferential access to Fund resources to the low-income developing countries would violate the principle of uniform treatment of members. They also argued that the Fund should not try to meet all the external financing needs of low-income developing countries. The Fund is a short-term to medium-term lending institution; its loans had to be fully repaid within five years (e.g., under the credit tranche policies) to ten years (under the extended Fund facility). Were the Fund to meet all the external needs of low-income developing countries for, say, three years under the extended Fund facility, it would then be placing an intolerable burden on these countries by requiring them to repay the loan fully within ten years. One of the fundamental rules embodied in the Articles of Agreement was that the Fund's resources were of a revolving nature and could not be used to compensate for a lack of long-term balance of payments resources or development assistance.

Most participants accepted the view that the direct purpose of the Fund was to promote a stable international monetary system and not to facilitate the transfer of resources from the industrial to the developing countries. Some questioned, however, whether the Fund could not, by introducing an SDR-aid link, promote resource transfer without impairing monetary stability. They argued that the link would not reduce the acceptability of the SDR as a reserve asset, would not aggravate inflation, and would increase aid. They noted that the United States could use its own currency to finance deficits and that other industrial countries and some developing countries could borrow at low spreads in the international capital markets. There was a third group of countries, however, that did not issue reserve currencies and that lacked creditworthiness. For these countries, most of which were in the low-income category, the burden of generating international reserves was very heavy and the benefits to them of introducing the link would be correspondingly very large.

Participants referred to the widely held criticism that the Fund's influence over the exchange and related policies of members was greater for deficit countries that used its resources than it was for deficit countries that borrowed in commercial markets or for surplus countries. They inquired about the validity of this criticism and about what the Fund was doing to produce evenhanded treatment of all its members. The Fund staff pointed out that the Fund endeavored to exercise surveillance symmetrically over all members. They recognized that the need of countries seeking access to Fund resources to engage in negotiations about their economic and financial policies did give the Fund the opportunity to influence these policies. They also argued, however, that the Fund had influence over the policies of those members that had a high degree of financial autonomy and suggested that the absence of recourse by members to competitive exchange rate changes was probably due in large measure to the Fund's surveillance.

Closing Remarks

Shang Ming

Ladies, gentlemen, and comrades: This has been a very successful colloquium. We who participated in it are most grateful to the Fund and the Chinese speakers for their addresses and for their responses to the many questions they were asked. As anticipated, the colloquium served well the purpose of exchanging views in a cordial and cooperative atmosphere.

I would like to highlight three subjects that appeared to be of special interest to participants: the economic situation of the West and prospects for recovery; growth and inflation in China; and the role of the Fund. Stagflation is now a major problem in the Western economies. Although the rate of inflation has declined somewhat, economic activity remains depressed and inflation is high. It is difficult to predict when recovery will occur and how lasting it will be. The view was expressed by some participants that stagflation is due to contradictions within the capitalist system and will therefore continue to be intractable. Another view is that inflation is becoming more manageable and economic activity may start to recover next year. According to this latter view, the medium-term prospects of the Western economies are quite bright.

The Chinese participants discussed the goal of quadrupling the country's net material product over the next two decades. They also discussed the issue of inflation in China. Some attributed this latter phenomenon to left-wing policies, others to excessive increases in the money supply. Whatever the origin, it is clear that inflationary pressures in China are quite modest compared with those being experienced by the Western economies.

With respect to Fund-related issues, many participants urged the Fund to give higher priority to the developing countries. Participants also supported the view that the SDR should become the principal reserve asset of the international monetary system. They believed that the uses to which the SDR can be put should be widened and that special attention should be given to increasing the allocations of developing countries.

I am very pleased that the proceedings of the colloquium are to be published, as this will considerably increase its influence.

Wm. C. Hood

Mr. Chairman, ladies, and gentlemen: I would like to express our gratitude to all those who have made our stay here both an intellectual experience and a personal delight.

I cannot mention everyone by name, but I would like to refer particularly to Mr. Shang Ming, whose interest made the colloquium possible. Mr. Zhang and Mr. Wang supported the project from its inception. It is impossible to express the depth and warmth of our appreciation to them for their efforts on our behalf. All of us have come to respect their wisdom and admire their efficiency.

It has been a pleasure for us to meet the various members of the presidium of the colloquium and our Chinese colleagues, Mr. Luo and Mr. Hong, who have presented papers at the colloquium. We have been highly impressed by the members of the IMF Division of the People's Bank of China and by the graduate students from the Bank's Institute. May I also express our appreciation to the interpreters whose excellent translations have made our communication possible.

The colloquium has been a success. I am pleased that we are now discussing with our Chinese colleagues how to disseminate more widely the ideas that have been presented and discussed by the Fund and the Chinese participants.

During our stay in China, we have sought not only to have intellectual exchanges but also to see something of your people, how they work and live, and to see something of the great cultural tradition that you share.

China has an important contribution to make to the world. It has a long and rich intellectual and cultural history. It has vast resources of manpower and materials. China's role in the world economy is destined to grow in the decades to come. The Fund looks forward to this development and will always be anxious to play an appropriate part in relation to it.

Azizali Mohammed

Mr. Chairman, ladies, and gentlemen: The time has arrived for concluding this colloquium. It has come much too soon, for we were just beginning to exchange the studied politeness of strangers for the give-and-take of debate among friends. But, perhaps, all events that are worthwhile have the same quality of ending sooner than one would wish.

We have been struck by the extensive knowledge of current international affairs on the part of our questioners, as well as by their intelligence and their sense of humor. We have been impressed by the attentiveness and unflagging concentration of this audience. Above all, we have gained valuable insight into your concerns about the world.

The following themes have recurred in the comments made by participants and the questions they have raised in the past few days:

—a deep interest in the prospects of the world economy and of China's growing place in it;

—an acute concern with the impact of the international monetary system on the developing countries and with how China as a developing country fits into that system;

—a particular interest in the adequacy of the facilities and services of the Fund in relation to the large balance of payments needs and indebtedness problems of its developing member states; and

—a critical concern about the equity of present monetary and reserve arrangements between developed and developing countries and the role that the Fund can play in fostering a more equitable system.

We have sought to explain two of the Fund's major tasks: the larger task of serving as an instrument of intergovernmental cooperation in an ever-changing global economic environment and the more specialized task of promoting adjustment by member states to that environment. We have emphasized the increased activity of the Fund in exchange rate surveillance, which has meant working more closely with its members in clarifying priorities, recommending policies, and facilitating mutual understanding of the implications of each country's policies—especially those of the major industrial nations—for the interests of the others. In the application of Fund policy to countries adjusting with its support, we have noted the large margins of flexibility in the prescription of appropriate solutions to take account of the circumstances prevailing in member countries and the conditions confronting these countries. In particular, we have noted that the Fund has not yet reached firm conclusions with regard to its approach to the centrally planned economies and that there must be a great deal of additional reflection on the basis of a growing fund of knowledge and insight before settled norms can be established.

Indeed, we regard the colloquium as an integral part of this process of study and reflection, and we are most grateful to our Chinese hosts for giving us the opportunity to exchange views with Chinese scholars and teachers of international finance and with the growing community of students in this field. This is a historic moment in the life of China, as it turns with an open mind to the outside world. We feel privileged to have been a part, in however humble a measure, of this moment.